Shine From Within

a teen girl's guide to life

Amanda Rootsey

HAY
HOUSE

Published in Australia by: Hay House Australia Pty. Ltd.: www.hayhouse.com.au
Published in the United States by: Hay House, Inc.: www.hayhouse.com
Published in the United Kingdom by: Hay House UK, Ltd.: www.hayhouse.co.uk
Published in India by: Hay House Publishers India: www.hayhouse.co.in

Design by Rhett Nacson
Typeset by Bookhouse, Sydney
Edited by Margie Tubbs
Author Photo by Bayleigh Vedelago

ISBN: 978-1-4019-5097-2

10 9 8 7 6 5 4 3 2 1
1st Edition, August 2018

Printed in the United States of America

For Trudi, my little fur baby.
Thank you for your unconditional love
and puppy kisses.

And Mum.
You're pretty amazing.
Thanks for always believing in me.
I love you.

CONTENTS

Part 3 Shine in the world

Our deepest fear is not that we are inadequate. Our deepest fear is that we are powerful beyond measure. It is our light, not our darkness, that most frightens us. We ask ourselves, 'Who am I to be brilliant, gorgeous, talented, fabulous?' Actually, who are you not to be? You are a child of God. Your playing small does not serve the world. There is nothing enlightened about shrinking so that other people won't feel insecure around you. We are all meant to shine, as children do. We were born to make manifest the glory of God that is within us. It's not just in some of us; it's in everyone. And as we let our own light shine, we unconsciously give other people permission to do the same. As we are liberated from our own fear, our presence automatically liberates others.

Marianne Williamson, spiritual teacher and author

WELCOME

~

Hi there! I'm so excited that you picked up **this** book. I believe that everything happens for a reason and this book has landed in your hot little hands because it was supposed to.

Maybe you're meant to read this then share it with a girlfriend who needs it. Maybe you're craving a bit of inspo to feel even more awesome within yourself. Maybe you've got a thoughtful person in your life who just knew you'd love it. Maybe a creepy person left it on your doorstep. How did they know you were a teen girl and would **love** this book? #stalkeralert Or maybe the reason isn't clear yet. We just have to be open to receiving.

I want you to realise that you are unique. Important. You might not realise it yet but **your life matters**. You were born into this world, at this exact moment, into this exact family (yep!), looking exactly the way you do, with the skills and wisdom that you have for a whole bunch of reasons. Those reasons might not seem clear to you yet, and that's the tricky part. But that's also the adventure.

You can do anything with your life and be whoever you want to be. The exciting part about your teen years is that you get to start exploring what's really important to **you**.

You'll make mistakes, no doubt. Like why didn't anyone tell me that my eyebrows were so bushy when I went to the school formal? The photos don't lie. But hopefully you'll learn from them too. You'll grow. You'll learn to forgive others and forgive yourself. You'll fight and make up a bunch of times with your friends. You'll realise that some of those friends aren't the best of friends after all, while others will be in your life for twenty or more years to come. You'll succeed and you'll fail. You'll play with your hair, fashion and make-up. (Even if you're not into any of that, you'll still make a decision to **not** be into it, which is a statement in itself!) You'll cry so intensely that you might fear you'll never be happy again and you'll laugh so hard that you can't imagine why tears would fall from those beautiful bright eyes of yours. You'll suffer and feel as though no-one else in the whole wide world could possibly get what you're going through.

And in those moments where it all feels hopeless and you're asking yourself, 'Is it really all worth it?!' you will find the strength within to keep going. I know life is hard sometimes. I know it can seem easier to choose a more destructive option sometimes, rather than trust your gut instincts and take the high road. I know it can seem easier to just go with the crowd. But you can do this. You can do anything. **I believe in you**. You are more powerful than you realise. You are stronger than you think.

DON'T YOU HATE IT WHEN BAD STUFF HAPPENS?

Wouldn't it be great if life was just perfect all the time? Perfect grades, kind brothers and sisters, parents who just say 'yes' to everything, good hair days every single day, sunshine 365 days a year, and maybe a little fairy godmother who floats alongside us each day and grants us wishes! Too much?

'I'm not a child Amanda,' I hear you say. Okay, fair enough. Calm down. Bad stuff **does** happen though, right? Like your favourite character being killed off a TV show. Or real bad stuff. Like a friend passing away. Illness. Break-ups. It sucks when things aren't going exactly to plan. Especially if you're a bit of a control freak, like I used to be. (Now I'm totally Zen, just ask my boyfriend. Actually, no don't.)

Here's what happened to me. Not that long ago, I was living what I thought was my dream life as a model in Europe. #fancy #modellyfe

On this particular morning, I woke up full of excitement, got ready, rushed downstairs and out of my apartment with a fleeting goodbye in a mixture of English and Italian (though I don't think it mattered because I was renting a room with an

Albanian family and I'm not sure if they spoke either language!). I walked along the Arno River in Florence, Italy, stopping at my favourite cafe for a custard-filled croissant and cappuccino, then walked across the famous medieval bridge, the Ponte Vecchio, to the Gucci offices for a casting (which is like an audition for models). But alas, my feet were too big for that particular job! Seriously, the things that you get judged on as a model are ridiculous.

I then headed off to the Salvatore Ferragamo building. (If you've ever been through a fancy international airport you'll have seen this high-end fashion brand next to the likes of Chanel and Louis Vuitton but were probably too afraid to walk inside! I still feel like that!) We had a big fashion parade there that day, showing the latest collection for the first time to the head honchos. Models were brought in from Milan to join us and I was pinching myself. An Australian girl, working in Italy, modelling alongside some of the best in the world. 'Is this real?!' I was thinking.

The show went well and I celebrated late into the night with the Albanian girls who had kindly rented me a room while I was living in Italy.

Next morning, I waltzed into my agent's office, a little worse for wear, but ready for the next job. I didn't want to disappoint beautiful Isobel, who had taken a chance on me and was finding work for me left, right and centre. She was kind, generous and always looked out for me. And this morning was no different . . . with concern in her eyes, she pointed out a lump on my neck.

'Oh, it's nothing. It doesn't hurt, so I think it might just be the way my handbag falls across my body—like it's rubbing or something. Nothing to worry about,' I said.

Fast forward a couple of months and I'm sitting in a doctor's office, back home on the Sunshine Coast in Queensland, Australia, being told I have cancer. I was 24 years old. I felt fine.

'What does he mean I have cancer? Seriously? Only old people with no hair get cancer but not me,' I thought.

That big scary 'C' word changed my life, but in the best way possible. Yep. It helped me realise how precious this life is. That things can literally change in an instant. It made me realise that we have to take care of our beautiful bodies—not bash them up for not looking the way we'd like them to or listening to nonsense from other people! Yep, nonsense. I said it. I'm old. Deal with it. :)

So what do you do when you're told you have cancer?

Well, in my case I cried like a baby. But first, I pretended like everything was okay. Sitting in a doctor's office, clenching every muscle of my body, focusing on not crying. 'Cause I'm tough like that.

I made it back to my car and balled my eyes out. 'What's going on? Cancer? How can this be possible?' I thought. And then I had to make the hardest phone call I've ever made to my mum, to tell her that her daughter had cancer. Stage 4 Hodgkin's Lymphoma was the official diagnosis I received later in the process.

And then I drove home. I had to just get myself together and take the next step. I didn't have time for thoughts like, 'Oh my goodness, what if I **die**?' and 'But why meeeee?' (Though I admit I had a pity party or two over the coming months!) In that moment, for the first time ever, I actually had to start taking care of this beautiful body of mine, before it was too late. Nothing else mattered.

It fuelled me to look at every part of my life and do what I could to help my body heal. That meant ditching the toxins (chemical-laden skin care, processed foods and even toxic friendships); embracing nourishing and healthy plant-based foods (seeya later instant noodles and canned meat!); getting my Zen on with meditation; and adopting a puppy (because what is more healing than puppy love?!).

I spent the next two years trying to beat this thing, doing whatever I felt was right to help my body heal and **trusting** that it would. I tried every natural remedy I came across and had conventional treatment too. Juice fasts in Thailand—fun! Radiation and chemotherapy—not so fun. But it all helped to heal this beautiful body of mine and in December 2010, just after my 26th birthday, I was told I was in remission. I've just turned 32 so am officially past the 'five-year' mark, which is a great sign that it probably won't come back. #partytime

During those two years, I was rushed to emergency more times than I can count. I wasn't sure if I would make it. I couldn't walk and at one point was out of breath just from standing for a moment. I had ulcers on both ankles and had to shower on a chair with my feet sitting on another chair out of the shower. I couldn't go for a walk on the beach or swim for **over a year**! I lost all of my hair (**all** of it, starting with pubic hair, which was a fun surprise).

There were some awful times in there, but I honestly wouldn't change it for the world. That experience taught me so much and reminded me of how quickly things can change. It made me reflect on my own teen years and say: 'You know what, Miss Amanda, you could've been a little kinder to yourself and your body.' It made me think about the type of world I would leave behind for future generations (I got deep) and how quickly time can pass us by. And that we should absolutely make the most of every moment, **truly shine from within** and embrace all of ourselves. That's how we help others. That's how we succeed in life.

There's a beautiful book called *Light is the New Black* by Rebecca Campbell. In it she has a chapter titled *You Do You*. She explains that no-one can do you the way that **you** can. And looking back, I spent so much of my teen years comparing myself to everyone else, instead of just finding out more about who I most wanted to be. Trying things. Embracing life. Shining. I want to share some of that with you in this book.

Because you're awesome. And I'm awesome. And because I believe that a lot of the reason behind why I got sick was that I didn't love myself and treat myself like I'd treat my bestie. And I got so caught up in pushing myself to be 'the best' and pleasing or impressing everyone else around me. I lost sight of what truly matters: the simple things like love, laughter and kindness.

So even if you read no further, please take a moment now to be grateful for the life you have in this moment. The people you love. The fact that you can read. The air you're breathing that the beautiful trees around you have purified especially for you.

You matter. You are beautiful. **You are stronger than you think**, even when bad stuff happens. And you absolutely deserve to truly shine from within.

HOW TO USE THIS BOOK

Firstly, be open. There is a Zen Buddhist concept of **Shoshin**, which means 'beginner's mind.' It means being open, eager and not having preconceptions when studying something—just like a beginner would, even if they already know about the topic.

So please take a moment now to commit to having a 'beginner's mind' and approach everything in this book curiously, asking yourself: 'What can I learn from this and how can I apply it to my own life?' Reading the book is just the first step; you have to take action if you want an awesome, shiny life!

A few tips to help you enjoy this book and spread the love:

- Dip in when you feel the urge or read it cover to cover—it's totally up to you.
- Read a little bit each night before bed, then whip out your journal to put any thoughts you have down on paper—so powerful!
- Read it and keep it for when you have a job interview, a special occasion, a problem in your life that you need to sort out or for when you just need a little extra inspo.

- Read it and then give it away to someone you think could benefit from it. Give a gift that can help someone else shine from within too. #goodkarma

This book is set out in three parts:

Part 1: Shine on the Inside is all about (you guessed it!) shining on the inside, because everything starts from within. We can apply as much make-up as we like or wear the latest fashion but, if we don't have the confidence to wear it and don't feel awesome on the inside, none of that matters.

Part 2: Shine on the Outside takes this confident, happy, gorgeous you and gives you tips to shine on the outside too, including finding your style, tips for glowing skin, make-up secrets and loads more.

Part 3: Shine in the World helps you share that beautiful, confident, shiny person with the world in a meaningful way. Finding your passion, helping you nail your first job interview and giving you the skills to communicate, so that you have besties for life who actually get you and support you. Let's hear it for the ultimate girl squad!

Throughout the book, you'll find action steps you can take under the heading: **Take shine-worthy action.**

You'll also find messages throughout the book from women in my life who I love and admire. I asked them to write some words of wisdom that they would share with their teen self. Consider them love messages from women who want you to succeed and enjoy this beautiful life.

You can think of me as a goofy but oh-so-loving aunty, who wants the best for you. Here by your side. My favourite thing in the world is to hold a space for teen girls to feel heard and understand just how much they **matter**.

So as you're reading this book, I'd love you to create that space for yourself too. Make yourself a cup of herbal tea, juice, coconut water, turmeric latte, beetroot latte, mushroom latte or [insert latest latte craze here], find a quiet space and dedicate this time to nourishing you. If you're sitting on the bus right now and a quiet, nourishing space isn't possible, that's okay. Just imagine yourself sitting on the beach, waves in the background, sun on your skin as you dive in to this book . . .

Part 1
Shine on the inside

I'm Okay, Aren't I?

~

Have you ever just sat and watched a little kid? Everything seems so wonderful to them! When they put something in their mouth they really swish it around, enjoy every moment and take time to decide if they like it or not. And you can see it all happening, almost in slow motion, on their little faces. They explore, they smile at everyone, they cry when they feel like it . . . they are just there, fully present in the moment, not worrying about a thing. Ahhh, bliss!

★ So what on earth happens as we grow up?

Do you ever feel like the world kind of grabs us, then twists and turns us, like we're being tumbled in a washing machine? Advice and opinions come in from all directions: questions about what you want to be when you grow up, pressure to do well at school and in life, pressure to look, talk, act and **be** a certain way to fit in. Have you ever noticed that people around you start competing, comparing and having all sorts of expectations of others and of you?

It's like we start judging (or forming an opinion about something), often without knowing all the details of the situation.

Then, as we continue through our teen years, you could even say that we start to live in fear. Fear that we're not good enough, that we might make a mistake, that others might think something negative about us or talk about us.

We start to evaluate happiness as something we need to 'get.' Does any of the following sound familiar?

I'll be happy **when** . . .

- I get a better body
- I'm in with that group
- I get better grades
- I move out and get freedom
- I get a job and buy what I want
- I have a boyfriend/girlfriend

Ahh, it's exhausting! In those moments, while we're wishing for something or someone else to come along and 'fix' our life, we miss a vital truth: that each one of us is perfect, right where we are. We are exactly where we are supposed to be. Deep down inside, we are just like that cute, adorable, loving, curious little kid, full of love. We're right where we are supposed to be and we're doing okay.

I want you to sit with that for a moment. You're okay. Say it in your mind, 'I'm okay.' Go to the nearest mirror, look yourself in the eye, smile and with all the love you can muster say, 'I'm okay.'

We've just forgotten how to live in the present moment. For example, you know what it's like when you're talking to a friend who's also doing something on her phone? You **know** she's not really listening, because she's busy somewhere else—maybe thinking about what she's going to reply to a text. So she's not fully present with you, she's on her phone as well.

Or other times we're the ones not being present, but no-one else would even know—it's all happening in our minds. Instead of enjoying sitting on the beach with friends, noticing how the sun feels on your face, listening to the waves, feeling the sand between your fingers and listening to your friend, you might be worrying about the exam you had last week. Or worrying about what to wear to an event next week. Or wondering why that person said [insert whatever random thing you wish they didn't say here] to you. Your mind is elsewhere, so you're not **present**.

Sometimes we're so busy trying to learn how to be an adult (and prove that we are responsible and 'adult' enough to go out) that we forget our special child-like wonder and awesomeness. We're so busy looking ahead or worrying about the past that we fail to stop, breathe and notice what's happening **in this moment**.

★ Take shine-worthy action

Pop this book down for a moment and notice where you are right now. What can you see? What can you smell? What can you touch? What can you hear? Take it all in.

Doing this brings you straight back to the present moment, and out of your head. It's a great exercise to do anytime you feel your mind spiralling or 'future tripping'.

SPRING-CLEAN YOUR HEART

Now, let's get one thing clear: recognising your own awesomeness isn't about bragging or being 'up yourself.' It's not about shouting from the rooftops, 'Hey everyone, can't you see how good I look?' #cueeyeroll

This is about knowing it deeply, within yourself, so that you can actually be present in life and support the people around you. Sometimes we get so stuck in our head, worrying about what others think, worrying that we'll look silly, worrying that we might fail. And then we never try anything at all. So, consider this your invitation to get to know more about yourself, so that you can show up as the most shiny version of you.

When you do that, you can be of the highest service to the world. You can really support your friends from a place of love, instead of trying your best but secretly feeling jealous. You can attract people into your life who make life magical and you can lift each other up, support worthy causes together and help others to shine, because you're already shining too.

So how to actually believe it within ourselves and become that confident, strong, smart, beautiful girl to our very core?

Firstly, we clear out the cobwebs. We take an honest look at how we see the world and let go of some stories that might be holding us back.

Then we get curious about the truth that's been inside us all along. We tap into our strengths and values and we honour the person we were born to be.

Are you ready?

★ Ooh la la . . . love!

Let's start with love. Ooh la la!

Ever seen a couple (IRL or in the movies) and thought, 'Oh, I can't wait for someone to love me like that!' Well, I'm going to let you in on a little secret so you can get any person you could ever want. And it doesn't cost a thing.

It's all about self-love. The key to attracting anyone you want into your life actually has nothing to do with other people. It's all about you.

So if you're waiting for Mr or Mrs Right to waltz on into your life and love you to bits, let me tell you . . . you won't attract the right person into your life until you **love yourself first**.

But you can start today and you can **share love** with each person you come in contact with, and feel love for everything and anything! Love isn't just for couples, it's all around us!

I want you to imagine filling your life with love. Not necessarily the romantic kind. The shiny, bursting with joy no matter who's around you love. Universal love.

You are so worthy of love, respect and kindness. Please find enough love for yourself and then follow your beautiful heart.

Trista Shanahan, naturopath and youth mentor, sharing what she would tell her teen self

A simple smile, assisting someone in need, preparing a yummy meal for someone, stepping over an ant on the sidewalk so that he may continue on his grand adventure, spending some time playing with your doggy—all of these are easy ways to share and experience a little love.

Oh . . . so just be a good human and be kind? That's love? Yep! And it's these **daily acts of love** that will attract more love into your life too.

★ Life is a rom-com

We can even invite love and happiness into our living rooms and watch it on our screens.

We can make a choice to watch movies and shows that are fun, happy and full of love instead of dark, violent and depressing ones. Ever had nightmares because of a show you've watched? Switch! And take notice of how the shows you choose to watch (or the books you read, music you listen to, even your social media feeds—but that's a whole other chapter) make you feel about life. We usually have more control than we realise over what we allow into our lives and how we see the world.

The other day my partner, Davey, and I were driving along and I noticed two people chatting outside a coffee shop. The way they were standing, the awkward smiles, the distance between them . . . I was convinced they were meeting for the first time, like a 'meet-cute' in a movie[1]. Davey said to me, 'You actually do see the world as though it's a romantic comedy, don't you?' I love that thought so, being the nerd that I am, I did a bit of googling.

According to Wikipedia, romantic comedy films (or rom-coms) are films with lighthearted, humorous plotlines, centred

---

1   A meet-cute is the moment when the two leading characters in a movie meet for the first time. See the movie *The Holiday* for a good example.

on romantic ideals such as that true love is able to surmount most obstacles.

Why not choose to see the world as a rom-com, rather than a depressing drama or bloodsucking horror film? Bad things still happen in rom-coms—they have their dilemmas and their challenges—but it always works out rosy and lovely in the end. The lead characters always get through their challenges and end up 'happily ever after.' I love that.

And here's the key, which we'll come back to over and over again in this book. It's a choice. We can choose to see the world this way. We'll dive into the science behind this and why it can be easier or harder for different people later in the book. Because it is actually easier for some people to be positive than it is for others, so don't be too hard on your mum, bestie or brother for seemingly seeing the negatives all the time. That could be their default. The cool thing is, if it's your default **you have the power to change it**.

> *When you're older, you'll find out you're on the autism spectrum. It will help you understand why you're so quirky, act younger than the girls in your class at school and many other mysteries about your life will be solved. We are all born our unique selves for a reason. Don't try to copy others, you're totally cool the way you are. Promise.*
>
> Kathy Divine, author of *Plant-Powered Women*, *Plant-Powered Men* and editor of *Australian Vegans Journal* on what she'd say to her teen self

★ love on steroids

While we're on the topic of love . . . find ways to spread love everywhere you go.

We attract what we put out into the world. So if you want a love-filled life, you can't just sit back and wait for it. You have to actively create it for yourself. Start by simply saying it:

✓ **Say 'I love you' more often.**
It's a nice feeling to know that people who are close to you realise how important they are to you.

✓ **Give a compliment.**
Ever thought something nice about someone but not told them? Why not? A compliment is such a simple but powerful gift. Share the love and actually let people know that you love their hair today, love their gentle nature, love how they can just get up in front of the class and share their thoughts so openly, love how thoughtful they are, love that they can make you laugh every day of the week. Tell them. Spread the love.

✓ **Say thankyou**
Next time someone gives you a compliment, thank them. I know it sounds simple but most of us tend to brush it aside, completely reject it or get embarrassed. For the person giving the compliment, that's like a slap in the face. So even if it feels strange at first, try to look the person who complimented you in the eye, smile and say a heartfelt thankyou. Honour them for taking the time and going to the effort of actually expressing something nice about you.

And above all, **love yourself**. Deepak Chopra, an expert in the field of mind-body healing and bestselling author, suggests that we 'replace fear-motivated behaviour with love-motivated behaviour.'

What that means to me is that we can choose to be motivated by **love** instead of fear and **light** instead of darkness. Or as my beautiful friend, author of *Mastering Your Mean Girl* and self-love expert Melissa Ambrosini says we can always choose love over fear to 'master our mean girl.' And when we choose to live from a place of love, we can face any challenge and are powerful beyond measure.

★ Take shine-worthy action

Decide on three ways you can invite love into your life, spread love and, above all, love yourself.

Here are some ideas to get you started:

1. **Invite love in.** Create a 'happy' playlist; watch more rom-coms.
2. **Spread love.** Tell your mum or dad how much you love them, even if it feels awkward; pick some flowers for your friend or sister.
3. **Love yourself.** Write a list of three things you love about yourself.

Start to notice what the little voice in your head says when you come up against something unknown. Does fear take over with messages like 'I can't do this' or do you choose love instead and give it a try? Choosing love doesn't mean you won't fail, but at least you'll know you've given it everything you've got.

LEAVE THE PAST IN THE PAST

Once I had recovered from cancer, I started to think about what I really wanted to do next. I didn't want to go back to modelling; it seemed a bit silly to me to help big brands sell a bunch of stuff we don't really need. It was fun at the time but it was time for a change.

I realised I wanted to share everything I had learnt with teen girls. I had spent a few years in my late teens and early twenties teaching deportment and modelling courses, so I decided to launch my own business and blend tips on how to look great with tips on how to **feel** great too. I didn't want to waste time doing anything I didn't absolutely **love**, so the courses and workshops I run are super fun.

One thing we often do right at the start of our programs is reflect on the past few months, writing down our achievements and celebrations, as well as anything that we're ready to let go of. These can be past situations that make us feel guilty or bring up feelings of anxiety, such as fights with friends or other experiences that make us feel sad or hurt. Things like:

- illness
- feelings of failure

- worrying about people or things out of our control
- a break-up
- self-sabotage
- not feeling good enough

And what we do with these situations is write them down on a piece of paper and then stand around in a circle and burn them in a beautiful fire ceremony. This involves a bowl, a candle and an adult (usually me) burning the pieces of paper in front of us.

This releasing ceremony is so powerful, because you get to actually watch those things burn up in front of you and that is such a healing experience. Instantly, I can see that the girls look and feel lighter.

> *You don't have to carry the world, and the problems of all those you love, on your shoulders. Sometimes they have to walk for themselves—and this doesn't make you any less loyal, supportive, loving, giving or deserving. You don't have to choose between taking care of others and taking care of yourself— you can and you will learn ways to do both.*
>
> Naomi Arnold, life coach and human rights activist
> on what she would share with her teen self

If we don't consciously choose to let go of the 'stuff' that upsets us from the past, we can end up trudging through life with a big, heavy garbage bag full of crap. It drips 'bin juice' as we walk along and gets heavier and smellier. We carry it everywhere we go and we keep adding our stories to it. Eventually it becomes harder to see the positive side of things, because we're so weighed down by all our garbage.

This is how 'fear-motivated behaviour' can take over, because we let our past stories dictate how we feel about our future. The smelly bin juice stops us smelling the roses right in front of us.

Sounds dramatic and a bit gross, right? But seriously, this is why so many adults have 'issues.' They can't let stuff go.

So what I'd love you to do is to try your best to let go of past situations that still bring you anxiety and negative feelings or emotions. If it's something you can deal with and work through then feel what you need to and move on. Don't let the past taint your life now. Make a conscious decision to live in the present.

'Well, that sounds great Amanda,' I hear you scoff. 'But it's easier said than done!'

How do you actually deal with negative stuff that is playing on repeat in that beautiful head of yours? Here are some tips:

- **Write it out.** Get a journal and just start writing. It may feel strange at first. You may not know what to write, but just start with something like, 'Oh hey there Mr Journal! I'm going to start writing in you because Amanda said so. Feels weird, but here I am giving it a go because Amanda's awesome and I trust her. I guess I'm feeling pretty annoyed that my supposed 'best friend' Bella (not Twilight Bella—a non-vampire Bella) said some pretty nasty stuff behind my back the other day . . . ' Hey presto, you're journalling!
- Grab a blank piece of paper and **write down what you're ready to let go.** For example: 'Feeling guilty about not speaking up while someone else got bullied at school last week.' Then rip the page into a million pieces and throw it away, while deciding that you will learn from this and make sure to speak up next time. You could do the burning thing that I mentioned earlier too but only with adult supervision, so ripping it up is much safer! #firesafety
- **Shake it off.** Shut (and lock!) your bedroom door, put Taylor Swift on as loudly as you can and shake your booty. It's so

freeing! No-one else needs to know that you're listening to Tay Tay. It can be our secret.

- Try your best to stop yourself each time you find that you are replaying the situation in your head and **switch your thoughts to something that makes you happy.**
- **Take action.** There are times when you actually have to confront a situation head-on. You might need to make a plan to go to school tomorrow and talk about what's bothering you with the relevant person. I know it's scary but **standing in your power** and sticking up for yourself is part of becoming a shiny woman. You can do it.
- **Talk to someone.** Sometimes you just need to find a trusted adult and chat to them about it. You can talk to your dog too, but I guess it depends on what kind of advice you want.
- **Get out in nature.**
- **Dilute your problems** by heading out in the world. Go to a cafe. See a movie.

Still feeling pretty down and upset? You might need to get more help from your school counsellor, a youth mentor or a psychologist. Reaching out for help and asking to talk to someone about your problems is a very 'adult' thing to do. We all need help sometimes and often it can help so much to talk out our problems with someone who's not part of our everyday life. They can give a different perspective and help you see the situation through clear eyes, without the emotion that we attach to it. It's not as scary as it sounds.

Even though you might feel as though no-one in the world could possibly get it, it's important to try. You'll be amazed by how getting stuff out of your head can make you feel lighter and shinier.

★ Take shine-worthy action

Think of three things you are ready to let go of. Stories that have been weighing you down. Then choose one of the options above to release them. I promise that you'll feel lighter, shinier and have more bounce.

Bonus points if you can get your friends together, read this chapter out loud, write down what you're ready to let go of and rip them up, shake it off, burn them (if you happen to live in a cold place with a fire going and have adult supervision) or release them into the ocean together. What a special bonding experience!

★ Be willing to change

Ever done something you're not proud of? In Year 8, I remember running away from a girl with my so-called friends. The girl we ran away from would keep trying to find us and we kept running and laughing. I still feel awful about it. I knew it was a mean thing to do, but I didn't speak up. Staying in that same cycle of inaction and going along with what others were doing only made me feel worse about myself. So I had to ask myself, 'How can I change this?'

We can't do anything about the past but we can try to be better today and tomorrow. It starts by being willing to make changes and then being gentle with yourself, as you try to create new patterns and behaviours that are more positive and in line with who you really want to be in the world.

IRL ➤ **Problem:** You might hang out with a bunch of girls who bully someone. You're the quiet one in the group and, even though you don't actually say anything mean, you feel guilty because you know deep down it's wrong.

Solution: You might choose to sit with someone else at lunchtimes, when you know it's likely to happen. You might choose to say something to your friends like, 'Hey, how about we lay off her for a while,' even though it's scary to speak up. You might choose to tell a teacher about it anonymously, so that you can help to protect this person being bullied.

Decide for yourself: What feels right for you? There's no shortage of people who are happy to give advice. Everyone loves to tell others what to do. It's human nature. But only we know what feels right for us. And there are usually a bunch of different actions we can take in any moment— one will be perfect for someone else and another might be perfect for you. You get to decide.

★ Take shine-worthy action

Is there one thing you feel ready to change about the way you react and respond to the world? Something you're willing to try to change? Write it down on the lines below or in your journal.

....

....

★ We can't change others (if only!)

Say your parents get divorced and this upsets you (obvs). There's not much you can do to change this actual situation. You can't change how your parents feel about each other or how they treat each other. But you can think about how it makes you feel and decide how you are going to respond to it. If you scream at your parents about it (totally normal btw), you might feel guilty about this later on. So if you were in this situation think about why you got angry, what you are upset about specifically, and try to express this in a more constructive way in future. Make sense?

For me, my parents getting divorced while I was finishing senior year at high school was huge. I was devastated and I didn't know how I should respond. I knew I was angry. I remember feeling as though Dad was leaving me personally, not just divorcing Mum. My friends were amazing, even though they didn't know what to say or how to fix it, just being able to chat to them about it brought us closer.

Over time, I realised that I needed to express to Dad how I felt. I had to tell him how angry I was and I had to share my perspective on things. So I wrote him an email. I didn't send it straightaway; I sat on it for a little while to make sure I really wanted to send it. I knew I couldn't take it back after I hit 'send,' so I needed to be sure. Then I went for it. To be honest, Dad didn't love receiving it. He felt hurt. So it took time for us to both heal and move past this. But I felt so much better having stood in my power and expressed what was truly in my heart at that time.

I'm a pretty introverted, quiet person and I'm a peacemaker. I **hate** upsetting anyone, so for me to even send it was a big moment in my life. But it opened up a dialogue between us, and Dad and I are now closer because of it. I'm not just wandering around being annoyed at him, carrying that in my garbage bag full of stories. If I hadn't done that, I probably would have this running story that 'all men leave' or 'all men do the wrong thing eventually,' when that's just not true.

It also made me realise that I can't change what Dad, or anyone else, does in their life. All I can do is manage my own reactions and respond in a way that I can feel proud of.

✴ Bye-bye judgement

Ever heard something and immediately gone into 'judgy mode'?

- Why did she do that?
- I can't **believe** she did that!
- How could he be with her?
- Why would Mum say that?

We often come to the wrong conclusions and our judgements are rarely the full story.

We all make judgements based on what we see, hear or experience, without ever really knowing the full truth. It's like we're seeing the world through our own unique set of glasses that are tinted by all sorts of perceptions and experiences from our own life.

As soon as you judge a situation or a person, you cut off understanding and interpret things according to **your judgement,** rather than listening or seeing things clearly.

Someone I really look up to and admire talks about this very thing. Her name is Heather Yelland. And when she's on stage in front of hundreds of people she puts on a pair of ridiculous sunglasses from the service station. You know the ones. They're enormous, wonky and not cool. And then she puts on another pair. And another pair. On top of one another so that she's walking around the stage with her head tilted back slightly so they all stay sitting on her nose. I'm pretty sure she wouldn't be able to see a thing!

Each pair of sunglasses represents a different story or belief that we have. They could be deeply engrained beliefs from our families, our friends, our culture or our experiences. Things like: 'It's really hard to make money,' 'Girls are weaker than boys' or 'Only skinny girls get a boyfriend.'

We usually don't even know we have these glasses on and we don't realise that we're seeing the world through tinted lenses. But these glasses impact on how we see the world and what we expect in life. For example, if we're wearing a pair of glasses that suggest girls are weaker than boys, then we probably won't try out for the soccer team or apply to be team leader on an awesome volunteer mission to a third world country (how cool would that be?!). That's because only a boy would be suitable, according to our dodgy service station sunnies.

So these lenses, these glasses, can **hold us back**.

Once we recognise that we're wearing these glasses, we can choose to take them off. One way to do that is by trying to be open and non-judgemental about situations. By asking ourselves: 'What would this situation look like if I didn't have that thought or belief? What's another way to look at this situation?'

We can even choose to replace them with the cutest pair of pink, love heart-shaped glasses, as Heather does when she talks about this topic. These glasses scream positivity, so the moment you put them on and see the world through these new, pink lenses, any dream that you have for yourself becomes possible.

 IRL ➤ Say you get a bad mark in a class, the teacher is a bit awful to you and you leave class devastated. You walk out to lunch, see your friend and wave but he doesn't wave back to you. In that moment, because you've had a bad morning, you might decide that your friend is annoyed with you and that's why he didn't wave. You start coming up with a whole story about it and having a convo with him, back and forth, in your head.

But if you rewind that story and instead had a **great** morning, you might see your friend and when he doesn't wave back you go, 'Oh well, he mustn't have seen me,' or 'Oh I wonder if he's OK.'

See the drama we can create all on our own, based on our judgements, feelings and reactions?

★ Take shine-worthy action

Try to see situations and things just as they are, rather than imposing right or wrong. When thoughts come up, consider what 'sunglasses' you might have on at that moment. This can help you be more tolerant and open.

We are all connected and there is good in all of us, but we have all been faced with different circumstances and tests in this life. Everyone has their own path to walk. And we can never really know what another person has or is going through that may cause them to act a certain way. It's something we always need to be working on, but I think it is important for us to try our best not to jump to conclusions or judge too quickly.

★ See the light in every situation

Rebecca felt like she always had to put on a brave face at home and at school. She grew up on a farm in regional Australia, spending most of her time with her dad and older brothers. They were traditional—she was taught to never show her feelings and just get on with life. At school she was like a mama bear, always standing up for her friends, feeling that it was her duty to cheer everyone up. She was like a self-appointed morale-booster.

But because she had worked so hard at being the 'strong, happy one,' she didn't feel like she could express how she was really feeling. She didn't give herself permission to feel and express all of her feelings. So she held them in. The problem was that it made her feel like a fraud.

In one of our courses Rebecca opened up, sharing what was really going on in her life and how she was feeling. Immediately she sat up a bit taller and you could see from her face she felt lighter. At the end of the course she said, 'Thank you for making me feel safe enough to talk about things I haven't told many people.'

The thing is, the only person stopping Rebecca from exploring and expressing those feelings in the past was her. It's scary, I get that, but in order for us to see the light at the end of the tunnel, we have to feel and express the sad stuff too.

Night is darkest before the dawn.

Situations or events that may, at first, appear negative can be great opportunities for us to grow and can often present something positive. Of course, crappy situations often just seem crappy at first, but with a little hope and patience (and a pair of pink heart-shaped glasses), you can always find a way to get through.

IRL ➔ One of our students, Joanne, said: 'Happiness is over-rated.' She went on to say that, 'The other emotions are just as important. It's important to feel sad when you feel like it, rather than squash those feelings.'

So true! We've gotta feel all the feelz. Sadness. Fear. Anger. They are feelings and are part of the human experience. They need to be felt before you can move through them.

> **So feel what you need to feel.** And even write it out or vent to your friend/mum/therapist if you need. And then look for the light.

★ Keep the faith

You can't connect the dots looking forward, only looking back. So trust the timing of your life, trust the process, have faith in yourself and the unique journey you are on. Everything will work out exactly the way it is meant to, and it will all make sense to you when it does.

Kirsten Morrison, life coach and youth mentor,
sharing what she'd tell her teen self

When I was in hospital having another round of chemotherapy, I shared a room with this lady. One morning, I felt well enough to get up and move around, so I went over to say 'Hi.' She wasn't exactly friendly. She had given up on life. 'What's the point of it all?' she asked. 'Why did we have to go through this? I can't believe I have to just sit here and wait to die.'

It was devastating to listen to and I was a little shocked to be honest. Even though I had my dummy spits and tantrums sometimes, I always knew in my bones that I would be okay. I guess that's faith. I just knew it. And so I trusted that whatever pain I was in at that moment wouldn't last forever. I trusted that there was light around the corner. And I did whatever I could to find the joy in that moment. Whether that was listening to my favourite song or eating something yummy—little things I could still enjoy. A constant reminder of this was our beautiful puppy, Trudi. Trudi showed up with the same love and joy every single day.

Seeing this woman with no hope and no faith broke my heart. At that moment, I realised how much of a precious gift it was to see the light in every situation.

So find your own glimmer of hope, no matter what's going on in your life. We aren't given anything in this life that we can't handle. That's what I truly believe.

> *We have to look at the bright side of the sun, in the bright side of the corner. Okay now, that's one of my secret teachings imparted to you. You know, that's how we keep happy and contented, and develop our creative talent and our positive, happy nature. We can't always expect things to come out the way we want. But we should accept things as God arranged them. That's always fun and surprising and tasty, you know? It makes life more interesting.*
>
> Supreme Master Ching Hai, spiritual leader
> and teacher of Quan Yin meditation

★ Take shine-worthy action

Think of a situation that wasn't great in your life and write it down.

Now find one positive thing that came out of it. For example, I didn't get the mark I wanted for biology. That was upsetting, but it made me more determined and organised the following term, which helped me in all of my subjects.

★ Flex your forgiveness muscle

I can hear some of you piping up already: 'But Amanda, someone hurt me and now I'm cautious. Isn't it dangerous to go through life being super naïve, pretending everything is rosy with my pink love heart-shaped glasses?'

I get that. And that's where forgiveness comes in.

Holding onto anger, resentment and negativity causes stress and makes it hard to live **your** life with love and happiness. So forgiveness is not about condoning the behaviour of other people, but simply giving yourself permission to move on and attract positive things back into your life. Make sense?

Forgiveness doesn't make it all better but it **helps you to move on** and, if you're forgiving someone else, it gives the relationship a chance to repair. It took time, but now Dad and I get on like a house on fire. I realised that I can't control what he does and decided it was more important for me to have Dad in my life than it was to stay angry at him.

★ Take shine-worthy action

So how do you forgive? It starts by **being willing**, even if you're not sure how you'll get there yet. You can't change the past and you certainly can't change other people, but you can learn from past situations and change how you feel about things moving forward.

Step 1: What do you feel like you need to let go of or forgive? Write a list. This acknowledges it and allows you to start being more aware of how it affects your day-to-day life.

Step 2: Next to what you need to forgive, write down how you will benefit from holding onto it. This is a trick I learnt from my life coach training. Ask yourself: 'What do I gain by keeping hold of this?' Perhaps by holding onto resentments, anger or hurt, you don't need to accept your part in the situation. Perhaps it stops you from feeling how hurt you really were, or maybe you get to boast about being the one who's 'right' to avoid dealing with someone. There will usually be a reason why you're holding on, otherwise you wouldn't be. If this is something you need to forgive within yourself (maybe you hurt someone else and feel bad about this), ask yourself: 'What do I need to do that will allow me to let this go?' Perhaps you need to apologise or journal about what you've learnt. We can't change the past but we can learn from it and we can make amends. You don't have to keep on suffering.

Step 3: Looking at your list (or one thing that you feel like you need to forgive), imagine letting go of everything. Imagine if these things didn't hurt you anymore. How does that feel? Write it down.

Step 4: Finally, write down what you have learnt about yourself from doing this exercise. Did you discover something that you could do to start making amends and forgive?

★ Ditch the toxic peeps

The next step in clearing out our beautiful heart, ready for lightness and love, is to make sure we're surrounding ourselves with beautiful, supportive souls. You absolutely deserve this.

Have you heard the saying: *We are a product of the five people we spend the most time with*? If you take a look around at who you mostly hang out with, do you like what you see? Are you proud to be like them?

If a relationship in your life is causing you more harm than good, then it's okay to find a way to spend less time with them. (Where possible of course—you can't break up with your parents or your siblings!)

I've learnt from hundreds of workshops with teen girls that pretty much everyone has done something awful to another person and has had something awful done to them. We all make mistakes and, if you have a friend who's upset you or done something out of character, then you might like to just forgive and move on. But if you're constantly being treated in a way that doesn't feel good (by a friend, someone at school, work or even at home), then you need to address it. Sometimes this can mean speaking up and finding a way to resolve it (which is hard but so worth it!) but other times you just need to get outta there if you can.

How to recognise when you're in a toxic friendship:

- You feel bad more than you feel good when you're around them.
- They put you down all the time.
- You don't feel like you can be yourself.
- They bully others and gossip every day.

If you think your friends tick any of the boxes above, then it might be time to find new friends.

We'll go into the details of how to deal with sticky situations in Part 3: Shine in the World. For now, remember you have a choice as to how you handle situations but also what and **who** you allow into your life. If something or someone feels toxic, yukky or squirmy in the tummy then it might be time to let that go. We'll go into how to make awesome friends in Part 3 under the heading #squadgoals (page 209).

IRL ➜ What if you have something toxic happening at home? If you have a parent who drinks a lot (or something else that makes being at home hard), find other people to support you, even if that means asking for help. It could be a grandparent, a trusted neighbour, an adult at school or a counsellor (give Kid's Helpline a call if you ever need to chat to someone or get advice—they are amazing).

Do whatever you can, within your means, to care for yourself. Don't hold it all in. Confiding in your friends, but also an adult, can help relieve the pressure. You don't have to deal with it all on your own.

★ Take shine-worthy action

Make a list of the five people you spend the most amount of time with. Next to each name, write down your favourite qualities for that person. For bonus points, tell them what you love about them next time you see them. #bestiesforlife #favouritedaughter

1. ....

2. ....

3. ....

4. ....

5. ....

Is there anyone on this list who doesn't make you smile? Even though it might feel difficult, do you feel like you could let them go and release that toxic situation from your life? Another option is to limit the time you spend with them and create a bit of natural space between you. Some ways to do this:

1. Next time the person asks to hang out with you, say something like: 'Actually I'm really busy at the moment with school/work/family [insert whatever is true for you], so would you mind if I get back to you later?' This gives you time to consider whether you'd like to hang out with them and it also gives you the space to suggest something you would feel more comfortable with. For example, you might be really happy spending some group time with this person but would like to limit one-on-one time with them.

2. If there is a person on your list who doesn't make you smile but who you spend loads of time with (I'm thinking like a sibling perhaps?), then have a think about what you could do to strengthen that relationship. Could you take an interest in something they like and ask to learn more about it? Do you need to be clearer about what you need from each other? For example, you might need to simply say, 'Beautiful brother, I love you but you drive me crazy sometimes. Instead of snapping at you, I'll try to ask you for what I need, like some time alone in my room. Could we try that?'

★ What's in a name: nerd or party girl?

*People often label you as the quiet one, as if it is a weakness, as if it is a bad thing. Some people just don't 'get you' and that's okay. Because one day you'll realise you're actually more powerful than you think. You are a quiet **strength** and there is beauty in that. Don't try to replace it.*

Haley Rodriguez-Holland, youth mentor, sharing what she would say to her teen self

Ever labelled someone or yourself? Of course, right? We all do it throughout life, but especially in high school, we latch onto some labels and perhaps label others as well. They usually start with 'I am' or 'You are.' This is just another form of judgement. It can help you feel like you belong and identifies who you are compared to others. It helps you go, 'I'm like these guys and not like you.'

Some labels could be:

- I'm vegan.
- You're a bully.
- I'm a nerd.
- You're a surfer.
- I'm mentally unstable or I'm sick (or perhaps even a constant thought or saying 'my illness' as though you'd be nothing without it).
- You're a party girl.
- You're a tomboy.

Or they can be 'I'm not' or negative statements such as:

- I'm not creative.
- I'm dumb.

These labels or statements might be 100% true for you or the other person at a particular time, but they're just one part of the whole. They're not what makes you **you**. For example, I am actually vegan and I love animals. I know being vegan is great for the environment and I feel good eating and living this way. So while it's true, and I don't mind telling people I'm vegan, it's not who I am. I wouldn't want someone to only see me as a 'vegan' and then treat me differently.

Story Time ➤ There's a Buddhist story about an elephant . . .

*A monk is asked by the King to show an elephant to a group of blind people. To some, he shows them the ears for them to feel. To some, the tusks. To others, the trunk. To some, the tail. To others, a leg. Then the King asks the blind people, 'Have you all seen the elephant?' 'Yes,' they reply. 'Well then, what does an elephant look like?' the King asks. Those who were shown the ears say an elephant is like a big basket. Those who were shown the tail say an elephant is like a broom. Those who were shown a leg say that an elephant is like a big post, and so on. They end up arguing and fighting with one another. But they were **all** right; they just only got to see one aspect of the elephant.*

Releasing judgement and labels is just like being open and curious to learn more about something or someone.

★ Drop the labels

When we label the people around us and ourselves, we create separation: 'I'm over here, and you're over there' or 'I'm this way and you're that way.' This makes it clear that we are different, which can make us feel either isolated (as though no-one else gets us) or over-dependent on the people we believe are the same as us and have the same labels as us.

The amazing thing with life is that we're all connected and we're all part of the whole. What affects you **does** affect me. We all have to poop, eat, breathe, sleep and a whole bunch of other things that make us human—regardless of the label we place on ourselves or others.

Understanding this helps us to feel compassion for others, forgive others more easily and feel less stressed.

So try dropping the labels! When you realise that others are not these labels at their very core, but that they just might be traits they are displaying right now, it's easier to get along with them. For example, someone who has bullied isn't a bully at the very core of who they are, they have just bullied someone. But they can change that behaviour and no longer be a bully. Make sense? And the same goes for you. If you're known as a tomboy, you can feel trapped in that label and feel like you can't make friends with girls, open up to girls or even go out and buy a dress if you feel like it, because you have become so attached to the label.

When we release a label, we suddenly open up a whole world of possibilities. A world of new experiences. This can help you feel less excluded too.

Research[2] shows that we feel less social exclusion when we understand this logic. When we realise that personality traits and labels can change and we are always evolving as people, we feel less stressed in a situation where someone has done something to exclude us.

A cognitive scientist at the University of Texas, Art Markman Ph.D, explains it like this:

Students who believe their own behaviour and perform-ance can change work harder in school to overcome academic difficulty. People who believe that others can

---

2   An article by Art Markman Ph.D in Psychology Today cites a number of studies: https://www.psychologytoday.com/us/blog/ulterior-motives/201406/the-danger-labeling-others-or-yourself

change are more likely to work with them to regain trust after they have a bad experience. Ultimately, it is important to realise that you should not completely define the people in your life by their current behaviour.

Cool huh?

IRL ➔ Feel like you don't fit in at school? Schools love labels and are pretty much set up to place you in a labelled box—academic, arty, sporty, etc.—and different schools value different things. If you feel like you don't fit in, you just might not conform and fit in to what they value at your particular school. There's nothing wrong with you, you don't need to change and you don't need to go to another school. Just find a way to make it work for **you**.

Embrace who you are and express **all** of you, not just one label.

Finding ways to express yourself in your own way, while also doing your best to be a part of the community you're in right now, will help you for the rest of your life. It's easy to go, 'I don't fit in here, stuff you guys, I'm out.' But the awesome thing about school is that it's generally a pretty safe place for you to practise dealing with a whole bunch of people, a whole bunch of rules and expectations and figure out how you can thrive in a bunch of different situations before heading out into the 'real world.' So . . . even if you're hanging to get out of there, consider changing your perspective and ask yourself: 'How can I make this work for me?' or 'Yesterday I had a bad day because this and this happened. Today I'll try this instead and see if it works.'

I still have the huge tree you painted, with all its roots showing, on my bedroom wall. Thankyou for expressing what you care about in your art and your diaries and songs. These activities are like secret tunnels back to yourself, a place where you can hear yourself better, when life gets confusing. They are your own special way of seeing yourself and this world, and that's very important. Keep loving, flower child.

Lisa Mitchell, Australian singer-songwriter sharing
what she would say to her teen self

Check Lisa out. She was on *Australian Idol* as a teenager and I've loved her ever since. #fangirl #borderlinestalker I LOVE HER

★ Take shine-worthy action

Have you placed any labels on yourself? What are they? How would it feel to drop them?

....

....

....

....

....

....

WHAT MAKES YOU YOU?

Now that we've done a bit of spring-cleaning of our heart and maybe dropped a label or two, let's dive into what makes you **you**!

You are you and there's nothing you can do to change that. Not even an invisibility cloak (or Polyjuice Potion for that matter) can change who's underneath. Think of your own beautiful self as a precious young girl. Discover her. Embrace her. Ask her what she loves and doesn't love. Try different things with her and see what lights her up. Because you and her, her and you—you're together forever. So, let's discover what makes her tick, what rocks her world, then build up her self-esteem and resilience.

Try this! ➤ Here's a little trick Kris Carr (cancer-kickin' author and movie maker) suggests.

Picture yourself when you were five. Better still, find a pic of yourself at that age! How would you treat her, love her, feed her? How would you nurture her, if you were the mother of little you? I bet you would protect her fiercely, while giving her space to spread her itty-bitty wings. She'd get naps, healthy food, imagination time and adventures into the wild. If playground bullies hurt her feelings, you'd hug her tears away and give her perspective. When tantrums or meltdowns turned her into a poltergeist, you'd demand a loving timeout in the naughty chair.

I invite you to extend this unconditional love and compassion to your older self—you are still that gorgeous little girl who needs playtime, fun, tenderness and a big ol' dose of self-love. And maybe a loving timeout sometimes!

★ What is self-esteem and resilience?

If you can dance and be free and not be embarrassed, you can rule the world.

Amy Poehler, comedian

If you're already rolling your eyes at the words 'self-esteem, resilience, and self-respect' hang with me here. Teachers and parents love to throw these words around as though the moment you get these, your life will be perfect. You'll be the epitome of the perfectly mature and sensible girl. Or worse, they might throw them at you like, 'Don't you have any darn self-respect?!!' 'Ahh no Dad, and now I'll spend the rest of the week showing you how little self-respect I have . . . watch me!!' you might be tempted to pipe back.

Let's explore these concepts for a moment, because a lot of what I'm about to share with you will absolutely boost your self-esteem and build your resilience. And by the way, this is a **great** thing.

Self-esteem is how much you like, accept and respect yourself as a person. To me, it's feeling like you can walk down the street, smiling at people around you without worrying what they might be thinking about you—because you're just rocking it and they're rocking it and it's a big old party. Sound fun? Great! When I ask my classes what self-esteem is, they say things like:

✓ how I feel about myself
✓ confidence
✓ being happy to be me
✓ liking myself
✓ being successful
✓ having friends

To give you an idea of what it's **not**, someone with low self-esteem might display the following behaviours:

× jealousy
× negative talk about themselves
× experiencing guilt
× failure to give compliments
× failure to accept compliments
× not taking their own needs into account
× not asking for what they want
× starving themselves of luxuries unnecessarily
× failure to give or receive affection
× criticism of others
× comparison of others
× constant poor health

Resilience is the magical ability to 'bounce back' when bad stuff happens in life (and bad stuff goes down all the time, to everyone).

Your own most resilient self is really just the self that gets by from moment to moment, not looking too far ahead and panicking, not thinking back and feeling bad about where you've 'failed.' Resilience is letting each moment open up to you in its mysterious newness. Letting the breathtaking abundance of life present herself to you, freshly made, over and over and over, this moment and this moment and this moment.

Dr Pamela Douglas, general practitioner and researcher

So building up your self-esteem and resilience will mean you can move on with life faster and not let the little things get you down.

Run your own race and leave your ego at the door— comparison is the thief of joy and bad attitudes are for schmucks. Keep being kind, polite, hardworking. These simple virtues will serve you well and take you places. Listen to your gut, trust in what it tells you and pay close attention to what you love and what you're good at. And that back brace you wore through high school? It will give you abs of steel, resilience in spades and the understanding that being able to laugh at yourself is a powerful gift!

Lise Carlaw, former international model and radio
host sharing what she'd say to her teen self

We can never have too much self-esteem. Yep, even that guy who makes you want to scream, 'Get over yourself!' If someone's arrogant, over-confident or bullying, then they are usually com-pensating for a **lack** of self-esteem. (I bet you can think of at least three people who are like this, right?) A confident person with a healthy level of self-esteem doesn't need to be boastful; they don't have to win all the time and they don't need the approval of others to feel good.

Our self-esteem impacts on everything: from the friends we have, whether we try new things, how we eat, whether we exercise, what we think and the words we use. Every thought and action stems from the way we see ourselves.

IRL ➤ We can always improve on our self-esteem and it's something we need to keep working on. **We can change the way we think and feel** and, in fact, we are the only ones who can do that. Our parents, friends and teachers can all tell us that we are amazing, but only we can control the thoughts in our head.

I spent most of my school years trying to be more extroverted, because that's what I thought my school valued. If you were good at public speaking, loved performing, were popular or were the sports star, then you were 'successful.' So I always pushed myself to do those things because, in my mind, that was the only way to achieve success and be liked and appreciated.

The problem with that is it's super draining to keep it up, if it's not really who you are. Self-help author, the late Louise Hay, said in her bestselling book *You Can Heal Your Life* that blood cancers, like the one I was diagnosed with at the age of 24, can be caused by 'a tremendous fear of not being good enough, a frantic race to prove one's self until the blood has no substance left to support itself. The joy of life is forgotten in the race to find acceptance.'

When I read that I was like, 'Yep, that was me!' Constantly wanting to be accepted at school, working my butt off with three different jobs while also finishing university, and then spending my days going for castings as a model, where you are literally hoping someone will accept you and book you based on how you look. #overworkedmuch?

But now that I know I'm actually quite sensitive, introverted and need more quiet time to myself and that my power and energy comes from within rather than from being around others, I have set my life up in a way that works for me. I get to work the hours I want to, create the way I want to, teach and mentor girls in a way that works for me and serves others the best way possible. I still love doing extroverted things, like speaking on stage to hundreds of people, but I can't do it every day and I know I need some quiet time afterwards.

> *Growing up I hated being so sensitive, feeling everything so very deeply, noticing and not forgetting 'the small things.' I wished I just didn't care and I thought being sensitive was a weakness. It wasn't until I did the Shine from Within course, that I realised that being sensitive is such a beautiful, caring, kind, amazing part of me. I now embrace it fully, instead of trying to fight against it. I now let myself feel things, I let myself cry when I need to let it out without feeling bad later, I let myself open up and talk to people when I think they need support and, most importantly, I don't hate that part of me. I love it! Allowing me to be my authentic self has brought me more self-love, more happiness and has made me more sure of myself and purpose.*

> Brylie 21, past student and graphic designer
> sharing what she'd say to her teen self

Understanding more about how you see the world, your strengths and your values can literally change (and even save) your life. If you don't know who you are or what's important to you, how can you expect other people to know? So let's dive in . . .

★ Are you a Negative Nancy?

Are you an optimist (see the world in a more positive way) or a pessimist (see the world in a more negative way)?

According to research shared in *The Happiness Project* by Gretchen Rubin, a person's level of happiness is determined by:

- approximately 50% genetics
- 10-20% life circumstances (age, gender, health, etc.)
- 30-40% how a person thinks or acts

Some people are just naturally born happier than others but, as you can see for yourself, that only accounts for **half** of the story. We can raise our spirits and increase our own happiness by focusing on how we think, how we choose to see the world and our life circumstances.

Think it's about **money and power**? 'Oh, but if I was born in **that** city with **those** parents who have all the money in the world, then of course I'd be 'naturally' happy, right? Wrong. Interestingly, one factor that doesn't have an impact on whether we're optimistic or pessimistic is how much money we have. Which is such a cool thing to know. It's not all about working our butts off to have more stuff in life. That alone is not going to make us more positive or happier.

Be honest, are you typically **positive or negative**?

When bad things happen, an optimistic (positive) person will think:

- It's just temporary and will get better.
- There's always something to learn from this.
- It's not all because of me, so I can keep trying to make a difference.

When bad things happen, a pessimistic (negative) person will think:

- It's permanent and can't be changed.
- This isn't the only thing that's bad, **everything** is bad.
- It's all because of me, and things always go wrong for me.

When good things happen, an optimistic person will recognise the role they have played and think it's normal that something good is happening. When good things happen to a pessimistic person, they automatically think things like: 'It won't last. It's because of other factors, not me, so I had nothing to do with it.'

> *When you start with the thought 'it will be okay,' you act very differently than if you start with the thought 'there is no hope.' Each thought is the first step on a different path.*
>
> Martine Sheehan and Susan Pearce
> in the book *Wired for Life*

Can you see the difference? Which one do you think you are? And if you think about your parents, do you think they see the world with more of a positive or negative viewpoint?

So what's the benefit of being more optimistic in our thinking? Well, optimistic people are more likely to persevere when things get tough, try new things and then experience more success, reinforcing their positive way of thinking. Whereas pessimistic people are more likely to avoid new situations, give up easily and then experience more failure (because they didn't try hard), which reinforces their negative way of thinking.

Which feels more shiny to you?

I look back in awe of your courage to back yourself and try new things—you're a rock star, and I love you.

Rachel MacDonald, business coach sharing
what she would tell her teen self

Our brain is like Google

What do you think happens when you google the word 'happy'? Lots of pictures that represent kindness, lovers, cute puppies, kids having fun, balloons and all sorts of happy things! Try it! And if you google 'sad,' you'll get lots of evidence to support that word. Dark images, sad events, just sadness by the bucket load.

From a psychologist's point of view, 'optimistic people will look for messages that support their optimist view; pessimistic people will look for circumstances that support their pessimistic view,' says Lyn Worsley in *The Resilience Doughnut*.

Without even realising it, a pessimist will be 'googling' negative stuff in their world—searching for all the things that show that things don't work out. And they'll get pages and pages of search results, because that's what they're looking for. Whereas a positive person will always be naturally looking at the bright side of life, because that's what they've googled. Make sense? Cool analogy, right? My friend and youth speaker, Katie Pitsis, shared this little nugget of wisdom with me!

The challenge is making that change. But now that you are aware of how your thoughts might be impacting on your life in a positive or negative way **and** you know that you are in control of changing those thought patterns, you'll be **shining from within** in no time.

Next time something happens, see where your head goes first. Does it search for all the reasons why it won't work or why that person **obviously** hates you? Or do you search for all the

WHAT MAKES YOU YOU?   43

ways to **make it work** or other reasons why that person might not have been so nice today?

★ Take shine-worthy action

Take some time with a journal or notebook and reflect on your day. What kind of thoughts have come into your head? Are they positive or negative? How could you 'google' a more positive version of things in your head?

> *You know this life? You got this. You got what it takes to get through **all of it**. You are capable of so much and you are so strong. You got this beautiful. You got all of it.*
>
> Allyce Martins, performer and youth mentor on what she would share with her teen self

★ Do you ever feel like your mind is spiralling out of control?

> *Remember that nobody can tell you what to think. Your thoughts are only yours.*
>
> Shas Patullo, youth mentor and also my aunty sharing what she would tell her teen self

Does anyone have mind control? Didn't think so. So who's in control of your thoughts, attitude and perspective? **Only you.** Well done.

As we have just learnt, how we feel or what we perceive in any situation will be determined by what we focus on (or google). The same goes with life. What you google is what you get. When you focus on being grateful for all the things that light you up and make you happy, you get more of those things. You find them, because you're already looking for them. Make sense?

One problem that can cause our minds to spiral out of control is when we start to google questions that are **not very helpful**, which often start with the word 'why'. For example:

- *Why is my life so bad?* Just like Google, your brain will come up with some answers. It might tell you that your life is bad because your parents are mean, you're dumb, your friends forgot about you, you're not pretty enough, etc. It will always come up with something, because you asked for it.
- *Why are my grades bad?* Because your teachers suck, because your sister annoyed you while you tried to study, etc. You'll find a whole bunch of reasons.

But if we switch this around to **how** and use the positive version of the question it changes everything. For example:

- *How can I make my life better?* Your brain will, like Google, come up with lots of ways because that's what you're searching for. Suddenly you'll see solutions instead of evidence that your life is bad: I can go for a run, ask Mum if I can see a counsellor, read a book, set some positive goals, create a self-care plan, etc. Got it?
- *How can I get better grades next term?* Study more, get a tutor, etc.

Can you see how that's so much more constructive?

✴ Take shine-worthy action

Come up with one question you could switch from a 'why' question to a 'how' question in your own head. Now write it down. See what answers come to you!

....

....

....

....

✴ What support do you have around you?

Self-awareness (aka knowing how we see the world and what's going on in our own head) is the first step to building up our self-esteem and resilience. The next step is acknowledging what support we have around us, what skills and strengths we have and what our values are.

These all build up a picture of what makes us shiny and awesome, which naturally helps us to start seeing that bright, optimistic view of the world.

So, who do you have in your life that you can turn to when you need advice? These could be people you're already really close to or people you'd like to reach out to and build stronger connections with. Look outside the box here. Some of our greatest friends and supporters in life come from strange places. Consider:

- family (parents, siblings, grandparents, cousins, etc.)
- teachers

- sporting teams (the coach, the parents who come to cheer you all on each week, your teammates)
- schoolfriends (and even students in other grades that you get along with)
- people you sit next to each day on the bus
- neighbours
- friends at work and even your boss
- people you connect with online

Once we start looking around us, we can often see that we have support in all sorts of places, even if we haven't needed to ask for it.

★ Take shine-worthy action

Make a list of the people you have in your life who support you to strive to be your best.

....

....

....

....

★ What can you do? (your strengths)

The aspects of yourself that you're labelling as 'weird' today are the very same aspects that you'll come to love and cherish most when you're thirty. Your weirdness is wonderful, wild spirit.

Tara Bliss, author of *High: A Party Girl's Guide to Peace* sharing what she would tell her teen self

Now that we've had a look at the way we see the world, let's get clear on our strengths. We've all got them. This isn't the time to cry, 'Oh, but I don't have any' in the hope that I'll do this for you. With this, as in life, you have to step up yourself.

This can feel strange. So often in life we find ways to express our weaknesses and play down our strengths so we don't appear 'stuck up' or 'up ourselves.' But in this instance, I want you to honestly consider what you're pretty good at. I'm not going to ask you to shout it from the rooftops at school. It's just for you. So don't hold back.

There are lots of strength-finder quizzes you can find online, but below is a short list of some strengths. From the list, circle strengths you think you have **and** circle the strengths that you admire in others. Go!

Creative	Authentic	Positive mindset
Curious	Honest	Detailed
Open-minded	Full of energy	Good planner and
Love learning	Kind	organiser
Wise	A good leader	Good listener
Brave	Forgiving	Dramatic
Persistent	Humble	Entertaining
Loyal friend	Funny	
Thoughtful	Hopeful	

Circle any of the following that relate to you too. People come to me for:

- advice about school subjects and help with homework
- advice about relationships
- someone they can trust
- someone who will be honest and upfront
- someone who will listen

- a new perspective
- someone who will remind them of the positives

It can be helpful to understand which traits you are not so great at, so that you can try to improve them. But that's not the focus here. One of the best ways to build your resilience and self-esteem is to hone in on your strengths, recognising that it's impossible to be great at everything but there are some things you're pretty good at already. And do more of those things.

So then, why did I ask you to circle some strengths that you admire in others too? Great question! Because sometimes it can be hard to recognise our own strengths and a little easier to point out what we love and admire in other people. The thing is though, **we only see in others what we have already within ourselves.** Read that line again. We see in others what we have within ourselves. This is huge. I'm not talking about how you like your friend's blonde hair when you have brown hair. But character strengths like the ones listed. If you love your friend's strength and honesty, then you would also have strength and honesty within you. Go you!

> You know that smile you see when people smile back at you? That's your superpower. You know when folks say 'gees you give the best hugs'? That's you showing up as yourself–high five her! Stick with her, she's fun, sassy and big spirited and you know what? She finds her people!
>
> Amy Cook, youth mentor and founder *Shining Hearts Everyday,* sharing what she would say to her teen self

It also means that when we get annoyed by someone, it's usually because it hits a nerve and it's something we have done before too. Do you get annoyed when your friend **always** turns up ten minutes late? It's probably because you have made people wait in the past, so it's something that is a trait within you too. Love it when your friend is thoughtful and sends you a message just when you need to hear some positive words? You recognise that as a strength within her because **you** are also thoughtful. See where I'm going with this?

So have another look at the strengths you circled for others. Can you see how you might also have these strengths too?

> *Stop trying to be like everyone else, be you.*
> *When you discover yourself you will shine.*
>
> Annwen Candy, youth mentor, sharing what
> she would say to her teen self

Extra Info! ➤ A lot of people waste a crazy amount of energy looking at what everyone else is doing. Comparing and competing. Keeping up with the people in the lane to their left and their right (imagining you were driving along a three-lane highway). But when we just keep our focus on our own lane, developing our own strengths and doing the things that light us up, that's where the magic happens. Stay in your own lane.

★ Take shine-worthy action

Pick out your top five strengths. Write them below and also write them somewhere that you'll see them regularly.

....

....

....

....

....

Now find two ways that you can use them more. For example, if one of your strengths is 'dramatic' find two ways you can be dramatic, like joining a drama club after school or starting a YouTube channel.

★ The big V: values are like foundation . . . or is that BB cream?

Values . . . these are the backbone of who you are. They are the foundation to your make-up. They are the bio to your Insta feed. They are the acai to your acai bowl.

They are what's most important to you. They are the thoughts, experiences or ways of living that we really believe in, cherish and try to live by. They often guide our everyday decisions in life, even when we don't realise it. They can even be what we want to be known for, or our legacy.

> *Don't worry, beautiful girl. Those wild dreams, that fire in your belly, and your resistance to obeying rules will become the greatest thing about you. Stay rebellious, stay determined, stay true to yourself, be a good friend and be a kind person. The rest will fall into place.*
>
> Yvette Luciano, author of *Soulpreneurs*, on what she'd say to her teen self.

When we don't live in alignment with our values, we can end up feeling unsatisfied. When we're around people who have very different values to ours, we can feel lonely.

So it's pretty important to get clear on our values. To do that, I'd love you to have a look at the words below for some examples of values. It's also important to remember here that there are no 'right' or 'wrong' answers and we're all different. So try not to think of this in terms of what your parents or friends might value or what you think you 'should' value. Just choose the words that really stand out and feel right for you.

Love	Knowledge	Nature
Peace	Popularity	Compassion
Success	Responsibility	Independence
Family	Spirituality	Academics
Loyalty	Beauty	Punctuality
Community	Fun	Spirit
Service	Fairness	Balance
Freedom	Safety	Creativity
Adventure	Health	Security

Another way to look at it is to start with what you don't believe in, like racism, cruelty to animals, etc. and work backwards. What things really upset you and get you riled up? Your values would be closely linked to this and be the opposite. So if you get sad about animal cruelty then 'compassion' might be a value of yours.

To explain this further and see how our values can impact on the way we see the world, consider this super scandalous story . . .

Once upon a time there was a woman named Abigail who was in love with a man named Gregory. Gregory lived on the shore of a river. Abigail lived on the opposite shore of the river. The river that separated the two lovers was teeming with man-eating alligators. Abigail wanted to cross the river to be with Gregory. Unfortunately, the bridge had been washed away by a heavy storm the previous evening.

So Abigail went to ask Sinbad, a riverboat captain, to take her across. He said he would be glad to if she would consent to go to bed with him before he took her across. She promptly refused and went to a friend named Ivan to explain her plight. Ivan did not want to be involved in the situation at all.

Abigail felt her only alternative was to accept Sinbad's terms. Sinbad fulfilled his promise to Abigail and delivered her into the arms of Gregory.

When she told Gregory about her amorous escapade in order to cross the river, Gregory cast her aside with disdain. Heartsick and dejected, Abigail turned to Slug with her tale of woe. Slug, feeling compassion for Abigail, sought out Gregory and beat him brutally. Abigail was happy to see Gregory get his due. As the sun set on the horizon, Abigail could be heard laughing at Gregory.

Who do you think is **most** at fault or in the wrong here? List out each character from the worst offender in your opinion to the person who is least offensive to you. There is no right or wrong here. The answers you come up with and why you chose them will give you an indication of your values.

I've read this story to hundreds of girls over the years and it always sparks a heated debate! This is because we can get passionately behind our decision, due to our values. For example, you might decide that Ivan is the worst offender, if you believe that your friends should be there for you no matter what. If that's you, loyalty is probably a pretty important value to you. Or you might decide that Abigail is most in the wrong because she cheated on Gregory, created a whole lot of drama and then laughed at the end when Gregory was being beaten up. So a few values there that could be important to you are peace, compassion and kindness.

There is both light and dark, good and bad in life. We can use our wisdom to choose the right path for us. Honouring our values, even when no-one else gets our decision, is tough. It takes bravery. But the gift it gives you inside is so worth it.

★ Take shine-worthy action

1. Read Abigail's story again and decide on your list.
2. Then read the story out to a few people in your life—your mum, your friends—and see what they say too. It's always different and that's the fun part. Everyone is right but it's a great way to notice how you see things differently and what might be important to people around you.
3. Write down your top five values and, for bonus points, **what they mean to you.**

1. ....

2. ....

3. ....

4. ....

5. ....

YOUR AMAZING BRAIN

~

★ Am I actually a crazy person?

Your brain and hormones and all that cool stuff . . .

Do you ever feel like you've got it all together one minute and are a crazy demon psycho the next? It's actually totally normal. Psychologists refer to it as the 'chaotic brain' because during the teen years your brain's development is literally jumping all over the place, from one side of the brain to the other. So next time your parents are frustrated with you, tell them that you are part child, part adult and tend to go between the two without realising it. 'It's called the chaotic brain, Mum. It's not my fault!'

And also, take it easy on your parents. It's a tough few years for them too as you turn from sweet little girl who looks up to them, to part adult wanting nothing to do with them and just wanting **freedom**, baby. Here's what's going on . . .

During puberty, the brain and pituitary gland release hormones that regulate the reproductive organs of both males and females. 'As a result, children begin to mature biologically, psychologically, socially and cognitively—a process that can take anywhere from one year to six,' says adolescent psychologist, Dr. Michael Carr-Gregg in the book *Princess Bitchface Syndrome*. Nice name for a book, right?

During this time, a few things happen physically for teen girls and not necessarily in this order:

- increased hormones
- growth spurt
- ovaries become active
- breasts!
- body hair
- menstruation starts

According to our favourite psychologists, Christina Leggett and Thania Siauw of Little Window Counselling, adolescence (your teen years) is also a stage of heightened creativity and emotions. The greatest amount of change that is likely to ever happen in your life and body is happening now. This can be great but also presents challenges, leading to feelings of confusion, frustration, loneliness, anger, sadness, shame and anxiety, not only for you but also for your family. So it's totally normal to feel these emotions sometimes. Thank goodness, right?

Just remember that high school is just a tiny tiny portion of your life and, in the years to come, you will struggle to recall details of all those little incidents that felt so significant at the time. Try to pick one great memory and one lesson in every day and let go of the rest. If you can't do either of those things in any given day, that is perfectly okay too!

Renee Bell, photographer and founder of *Little Girls with Great Big Dreams* on what she'd share with her teen self

★ The science

Our brain is made up of 100 billion neurons or nerve cells.[3] At birth, only about 17% are interconnected. [4] Over the next twenty years or so, the brain continues to form connections in bursts. The brain is constantly evolving, letting go of old connections that no longer serve and building new ones. In fact, the brain you woke up with this morning is not the same as the brain you have now.[5] #sofreakincool That must be why I forgot algebra the moment the exam was over! #whoneedsit???

The brain is comprised of two halves, the right and left cerebral hemispheres. While science is always discovering new things about how our brain works, the current wide-spread belief is that different functions, competencies and skills tend to be located in different areas. Specifically, language, writing, logic and mathematical skills seem to be located in the left hemisphere, while creativity, fantasy, artistic and musical skills seem to be located in the right hemisphere. Although the hemispheres may have separate functions, these brain masses almost always coordinate their functions and work together, though this is still developing during the teen years.

It's believed that until your teen years, development usually happens mostly on one side of the brain. For example, from ages 4-6 the left brain is activated more with a focus on developing language and problem-solving. Then from ages 6-9 it switches back to the right side, with a focus on social skills, connection and identity. But from ages 10-25, there is a lot of development happening in both sides of the brain, at times working together

---

3   Sheehan, M and Pearce, S (2012) *Wired for Life: Retrain Your Brain and Thrive*, Australia, Hay House.
4   Carr-Gregg, M (2006) *Princess Bitchface Syndrome*, Australia, Penguin Group.
5   Arden, John B. (2010) *Rewire Your Brain: Think Your Way to a Better Life*, New Jersey, John Wiley & Sons.

and at other times competing with one another. Hence the chaotic brain![6]

Another part of the brain is also forming during the teen years: the prefrontal cortex. This is the centre for reasoning and problem-solving and is not fully developed until our early twenties. This means that you, right now during your teen years, can be typically more impulsive and react automatically, rather than thinking things through logically. You may not be able to fully comprehend the consequences of your actions.

Plus . . . your hormone changes often encourage thrillseeking behaviour.

Plus . . . your life tends to run at a fast pace, with rapid changes and many 'firsts.' You are probably craving independence and **freedom**, while also really wanting safety and guidance.

So there's a lot going on!

★ Take shine-worthy action

Be gentle with yourself—your beautiful brain is literally going all over the place.

Show this chapter to your parents and, if you need, come up with a plan for when you go into crazy demon psycho mode. Maybe your parents could ask you what you need in that moment? Maybe you could have a code word (because no-one likes to be told when others think they're being a bit crazy!) and then when you hear that word you go for a walk or go to a quiet place and do some deep breathing (lots of great apps to help you with this too).

---

6   Siauw, T and Leggett, C. "Module 2, Video 5: Guest teacher interview with psychologists." *Youth Mentor Training*, by Shine From Within, 2016.

BUILDING BLOCKS TO SHINE

~

★ *What colour do you feel?*

We had a beautiful student in one of our courses, let's call her Luna. (She loves Harry Potter and I think she'll be a bit chuffed when she sees I've named her Luna!) Luna was the 'loud one' as soon as the course started—she had this ability to instantly make others feel more comfortable and loosen up, because she goofed around and made everyone laugh. Such a special gift. But Luna, like all of us to some degree, also had a dark side. She struggled with depression and anxiety (though you wouldn't know it from the outside).

She'd had a rough few months and had been seeing a psychologist, who she lovingly referred to as Tinkerbell, due to her pixie-like, magical ability to help her through tough times. Luna and Tinkerbell were obviously a great duo, because Luna was able to explain so many things to all of us in the simplest way—complicated things about our emotions and how we attract different people into our lives based on the energy we're putting out into the world. So I wanted to share this with you.

Luna explained that she sees emotions and rates how she's feeling based on colours. Some days she has grey days, or dark green, baby poo-coloured days. These are her more negative or sad days. At other times she has pink and orange days, 'Like a beautiful sunset shining out of me.' The cool thing is, Luna explained that we can turn on our own lamps inside of us and that whatever colour we are glowing, we'll attract other people with the same colour too. She said that when we turn on, for example a pink lamp, then a cord will instantly connect her with other pink lamps and they'll be attracted into her life.

★ Take shine-worthy action

Have a think about your own emotions and colours. Come up with a colour for these emotions:

- happy ....

- powerful/strong ....

- sad ....

- grumpy ....

- peaceful ....

(and any others you feel like doing)

As one of our beautiful youth mentors, Renee Bell, reminded me the other day, some people feel like black is sad while others might feel like black is powerful! So choose colours that feel right for you. It's such a powerful way to recognise how you're feeling and, if it's a colour or emotion that you don't want to feel, you can decide to do something to help you feel like your happy/powerful/peaceful colours. You can also use your happy/

powerful/peaceful colours to decorate your bedroom, wear in your clothes or make-up, etc.

★ Be your own best friend

> *Be your own best friend. You are perfect,*
> *whole and complete exactly the way you are.*
> *Self-love is the best self-compassion.*
>
> Melissa Ambrosini, self-love teacher and author of *Mastering Your Mean Girl* on what she'd share with her teen self

Make a pact . . . with yourself! When you're at school, it can feel like nothing else exists. As though the friends there are the only friends you'll ever have. But the truth is, friends will come and go throughout your life. Lovers will come and go. Teachers will come and go. And you know what? Only **you** can create the life you want. No-one else is going to be able to do that for you.

So make a pact with yourself to be your own supportive friend and give more to **you**. From treating your body like the temple it is to giving yourself some words of encouragement when you need it. It's time to step up and **start loving you**.

★ Take shine-worthy action

1. If you have a think about your friendships or family, what are some of the things you have done to support the people you love most in your life?

....

....

....

....

....

What would it look like if you did those same things **for yourself?**

2. Give this a go . . .

Go on dates, **with yourself!** Plan the most fun thing you can think of to do with yourself. Some people are just pros at hanging out in their own space, while others (like me when I was younger) have never spent any time on their own. I know I had never even been home alone without needing to have the radio or TV on, so that I felt like there was company.

It will feel totally strange at first, but if you can do one thing all on your own and enjoy life without needing others some-times, you'll feel stronger in who you are and will find some quiet. And it's in the quiet that you get the **best** ideas and get to know what you like and don't like. It will also make you a better friend and partner, because you'll be right there **with them** when you're together, instead of depending on them to make you happy.

★ *#Grateful*

Having gratitude and feeling thankful shifts your focus from what you don't have to all the wonderful blessings that you do have. It's like constantly googling happiness, because you're focusing on the good stuff, which attracts more good stuff.

How do we get an attitude of gratitude? You can start by saying, 'I'm thankful for . . . ' and then list out all the things you are thankful for in your life. This can feel tricky at first, but once you get into the swing of it, it's a cinch.

Here are some ideas to get you started. I'm thankful for . . .

- sunshine
- a roof over my head
- clean water
- my best friend
- my new favourite jeans
- chocolate
- puppy love
- glasses, so I can read
- legs that take me on fun adventures
- my tongue, so I can taste my favourite foods
- my smile, so I can show others when I'm happy
- the beach
- the trees that purify the air for us to breathe
- family dinners
- wi-fi
- teachers who care about me
- the chance to even go to school
- paint brushes
- rom-com movies
- angels/fairies/mermaids (or whatever you believe in) watching over me

The best way to practise gratitude is to find a way to do it daily, because it's on the days when you don't think about it (or certainly don't feel like it) that you probably need it most. So you need to make it a habit.

★ Take shine-worthy action

Get yourself a journal or notebook and write down three things you're grateful for today. The sun, the stars, your mama, your bestie, the grass under your feet, Netflix . . . whatever. Do this every day. Call it your gratitude journal.

Come up with new ones all the time. (It gets old quickly if you just list the same three every day!)

★ Habits that actually stick

Speaking of habits . . . they are regular, routine behaviours we do in our lives, often without needing to think about them.

We have great habits as well as not so great habits. For example:

- brushing your teeth every night before bed (great!)
- saying 'I love you' at the end of a phone call to your mum (great!)
- taking your dog for a walk most mornings before school (great!)
- tuning out as soon as your little sister talks to you (not so great)
- biting your nails when you're nervous (not so great)
- scrolling through social media on your phone before bed (not so great)

The thing is, we can learn to change the not-so-great habits and create new ones. According to Leo Babauta, creator of the blog *Zen Habits*, the key to making lasting changes that become habits is:

1. doing them consistently
2. not trying to change too much at once
3. picking a trigger

A trigger is something you already do, something that's already ingrained in your routine. You can use this as the anchor for new change. For example, you might decide you want to get out for a walk each morning. To anchor it in, you might decide that you will go for a walk right after drinking your morning smoothie (the trigger). So each time you drink your smoothie, you'll remember to go for your morning walk!

It's widely believed that it takes around 28 days to form a new habit, so you need to stick with it for at least that long. And the longer the better, to really cement the new habit into your life.

★ Take shine-worthy action

Are there any habits you would like to let go of or create at the moment? Write them down.

....

....

....

How can you anchor these into your daily routine?

....

....

....

★ How to build your own self-esteem

When I was coming into high school, I found it really difficult to look at myself in the mirror and say I was happy with how I looked. So what I did was I would go for a run and, when I got back all sweaty with messy hair, I would stare at myself in the mirror and

say 'you are so beautiful' and I would just repeat
that over and over again. I also found it difficult to
sort of figure out who I was, so what I did was make
an inspiration board and stuck any magazine clip-
pings, book quotes, beautiful colours, cool fabrics
or flowers onto this board and whenever I was
feeling down I would look at it and remember what
made me happy. I would take a deep breath and
lift my head and jump back into life head first.

Montana 16, past student, sharing what's helped her as a teen

Feeling great all the time is pretty much impossible. And it's okay by the way. Sometimes we're sad and we need to be sad. Then we need to pull ourselves out of it.

So to recap, it starts with understanding more about what makes you **you**. All the stuff we've discussed already like your strengths and your values—that's what builds your self-esteem. But knowing them is only half of the equation. You have to put things into practice. You have to find ways to **use your strengths and skills**. You need to make decisions based on your values, so you feel like you're **living your truth**.

Just like Montana, you have to commit to doing things that build up your self-esteem, like her inspiration board idea and saying, 'You are so beautiful' to yourself in the mirror.

Some ways to feel good about yourself:

- Recognise your strengths and values—tick!
- Accept compliments gracefully.
- Give compliments sincerely.
- Always speak well of yourself and others (try not to gossip).
- Praise yourself. If you do something good, it's okay to feel good about that—you don't have to shout it to the world but it's nice to acknowledge your accomplishments. Especially

if the people in your life don't tend to praise you automatically. Be your own cheerleader!

- Treat your body well and feed it healthy, live, nourishing foods.
- Forgive yourself. If you do something that you are not proud of, learn from it and forgive yourself—we all make mistakes.
- Surround yourself with people who treat you well. You deserve a nice group of friends.
- Practice gratitude—tick!
- Get yourself a card deck of inspirational quotes. Or make one yourself!
- Have a list of your favourite YouTubers who always make you laugh, for those days that don't feel great.
- Download and fill in the 'Building Blocks to Shine' worksheet from my website shinefromwithinhq.com so you have a list of all the things you can do when you feel sad.
- Get out in nature: feet on the grass or sand. Yum!
- Create a playlist of all your favourite happy, mood-boosting songs. You can also find links to our custom 'Happy' or 'Peaceful' playlists on the website.
- Do something for someone else.

DREAM a LITTLE DREAM

Do you have a dream? Something you'd love to see in your life, experience or create? It could be a big dream or a small dream. Even if it seems impossible, I know for sure that **you can achieve whatever you want to in life.**

Hey, I never thought I'd be modelling in Europe, but I got to do it! And to be honest, I worked hard for that; I was rejected a few times by my agency before they even took me on, but I didn't give up. Then when I graduated from uni and had already been modelling in Australia for a few years, I was ready to go exploring. I thought, 'Wouldn't it be awesome to go travelling and earn money as a model on the way?' Why not, hey? So I put some images up of me in fashion parades next to pictures of other models in big fashion parades in Europe. I put these pictures on the door of my wardrobe, so I would look at them a few times a day and see myself modelling alongside other models in Europe. Like a mini vision board.

Then I walked into my agency and told them my plan. They shut it down pretty quickly and said I would need to move to another city in Australia first and only then could I go overseas. I didn't want to do that, so I asked them to set up some meetings for me anyway . . . 'because I'm going!' Sometimes you have to be firm!

Mum and I set off to Germany for a holiday and I went to some meetings. I then set up a bunch of extra meetings myself and went along to those as well. Within a couple of weeks, I had found myself an agency. From there I found my own way, getting another agency in Italy too.

If I had taken that initial 'no' from my agency, then I would never have had that awesome experience overseas. And by the way, even if I hadn't got an agency over there, I'm sure I would have found another job, stayed and had the best time anyway. Sometimes things don't necessarily turn out as planned, but having the dream in the first place is what gets us moving forward.

A few things to keep in mind about dreams:

- **Dreams can change**, and that's okay. If you want to be a rock star today and an astronaut tomorrow, then go for it! They don't have to be 'lifelong' dreams. And if you decide you no longer want to do something, then it's okay to stop doing it. Sometimes dreams just morph into something different. That's the magical thing about dreams!
- **Keep them safe** and protect them. One of our guest teachers, Kaye Vlachos, who represented Australia in soccer, shared this with our students one day and I've never forgotten it. You don't have to shout your dream from the rooftops, you don't even have to share it with your bestie. Keep it safe and only share with those who will support you to achieve it. (No-one needs a Negative Nancy telling you it's not possible–boring!)
- Dreams can only be achieved if you **set goals and actively work towards them**. You can't get sad about not being a famous ballerina if you can't be bothered going to dance class. Dreams take dedication.

★ Be your own life coach!

*Dream big, girl, and take small daily steps
towards it. Don't quit! You are here not
to be **the** best but to be **your** best.*

Renee Frost, youth mentor, sharing what she'd tell her teen self

Set goals for yourself, check in with yourself and celebrate the wins!!!

Goal setting is amazing. A dream can feel really hard to achieve, but once you turn it into a goal and set some little action steps, suddenly it's possible and you're on your way! You can create goals for any area of your life, such as your fitness and health, family and friendships, academic performance, spirituality, finances, business, creativity, self-development—they all follow the same process.

There are lots of different goal-setting tools you can use but, as a trained life coach myself who has coached many girls, I can tell you that feelings-based goals work best. So first we've got to tap into how you feel now about different areas of your life and how you want to feel.

Step 1: How do you feel about different areas of your life?
Grab your journal and list out a few different areas of your life, such as:

- friendships
- family
- academic performance
- creativity
- health/body
- self-worth

Next to each one write down what **colour** you feel about that area of your life right now and any notes that come up for you as you decide this (see Page 50 about colour). If you prefer numbers to colours, you could rate them each on a scale of 1-10, with 10 being **great**.

Step 2: How do you want to feel?

Forget the 'how' of achieving it for a moment and just focus on how you **want to feel** in each area of your life and how you want to feel on a regular basis. In your list, add the colour that you would like to feel and also a word that represents how you want to feel. For example, you might want to feel **energetic** in your body. Or **strong**. Or **beautiful**. Deciding on how you want to feel is much more powerful than simply stating: 'I want to be more fit.' Ever tried to stick to one of those goals? They don't stick and don't work, because you haven't anchored into why you want to achieve it in the first place. So, get clear on how you want to feel.

Step 3: Let's set your goals

Forget the SMART acronym. We want your goals to be so much more than that. According to the Beautiful You Coaching Academy, your goal needs to be:

- **Inspirational**—does it make your heart flutter?
- **Positive**—make sure it's something positive to work towards, rather than to 'stop' doing something. Find the positive. We're more successful working towards something we want, rather than trying to move away from something we don't want.
- **Emotive**—it should make you feel something. So instead of 'I want to get three As next term,' it could be 'feel proud and celebrate my best effort ever at the end of next term.'
- **Challenging**—it should be a little out of your comfort zone and 'stretch' you just a bit.

- **Achievable**—while challenging and stretching it should still be possible, so think about how much time and resources you have.
- **Focused**—is it focused on one thing? If you've got a few things that come to mind that you'd like to achieve and they all relate to one another, what's the **main goal** that you'd like to achieve? The rest could be steps or actions you take.
- **Measurable**—we have to be able to measure it. So think about this: how will you know when you've achieved it?

An example goal: **I want to feel the most self-confident I've ever felt by spring.** It's inspiring, positive, emotive, challenging, achievable, focused and we'll be able to measure it as we go through the following steps.

Step 4: What's your starting point?

Once you've got your goal written down, you want to get clear on what it means to you and exactly how you feel about this area of your life now. So you might spend a week or two taking notice of when you already feel self-confident and when you don't. Use your journal to check in with how you're feeling each day.

Step 5: What's the most inspiring vision you can create for yourself now?

Now we want to create a vision for this goal. Using the example goal above, what does it look like for you to be the most self-confident version of yourself? What would you be doing? Who would you be spending time with? What would you wear? What would you try? What does that girl, who is the most self-confident she's ever felt, feel like? Most importantly, know that you have everything you need, you are worthy of this and all the tools you need will come to you for you to live a happy life. You can even create a vision board for your goal, using an app like Pinterest, or old-fashioned cardboard, paints and magazines.

You could add pictures of girls running on the beach, speaking in front of a class, surrounded by friends—whatever inspires you to be the most self-confident you've ever been.

In order to carry a positive action, we
must develop here a positive vision.

His Holiness, the 14th Dalai Lama

Step 6: What could get in your way?

List any obstacles that could get in the way of achieving your goal and how you can overcome them. Taking time to plan for this will help you keep going when an obstacle arises.

Step 7: What are all the things you need to do to achieve this goal?

Now that you've created a vision for yourself, list out your action steps for achieving this goal. You could even think of your goal as a beautiful island destination and all the action steps happen while you're on the boat on your way over there. Sometimes the boat might have to swerve to avoid a dolphin playing in the water, or go in a different direction for a while because a storm is coming, but then it will get back on track and finally end up in paradise. For some goals, your boat will be a speedboat or maybe you'll just catch a helicopter there and be celebrating by dinnertime! For other goals, you might be rowing yourself there, so you'll need plenty of breaks and maybe a little swim over the side before you keep going. Either way, you'll get there.

I really love to get a big sheet of paper and draw the little island at the top of the page, writing the goal in it or next to it. And then I list the action steps in the water below. Make sure you break them down into super simple steps. Some action steps for this particular goal could be:

- Write out my strengths and put them on my wall, so I remember to use them.
- Research inspiring books.
- Choose one book and hire it from the library or buy it.
- Read the book!
- Go through my cupboard and decide on three outfits that make me feel confident.
- Read out affirmations to myself in the mirror each morning (eg. I am beautiful, smart and have everything I need within).
- Find three potential jobs I can apply for (because getting a job can increase your confidence).
- Apply for those jobs.
- Turn up to the interviews, even though it feels scary.
- Create a self-care menu for myself including having a bath once a week, learning to meditate and walking three times a week.
- Practise speaking up with my friends and family.

Step 8: Order your steps and give them a timeline

Give yourself a reasonable deadline for each one and check in with yourself each week, to see what you've achieved and how you're feeling.

Step 9: Celebrate your achievements!

Then finally, let go of the outcome. I know that sounds crazy. But stick with me. I believe that everything happens for a reason. I believe that the universe has my back. And I can tell you from experience that when we set a goal and work towards it, we may not achieve it the way we expected to. But what often happens is that the universe provides an **even better** alternative than we ever could've dreamed up. But if we're too busy being sad or stressed because what we expected didn't happen, then we'll never get to enjoy those unexpected riches.

To illustrate this point, think about your goal of being the most self-confident you have ever been. In the beginning, you might think that means you'll be able to speak in front of the class and that's what it's all about for you. But as you go along, doing your action steps and feeling more confident, you might find you end up with a new bunch of friends who love and support you. Be open to where life takes you. By setting feelings-based goals, you can achieve them in a range of different ways.

★ Take shine-worthy action

Pick three areas of your life that you'd like to set a goal in. Go through the process above to set three goals.

NOURISH FROM THE INSIDE OUT

Okay. Let's talk about your body. It's the only one you've got. It's your magical vehicle here on planet Earth so that you can do, be, say and create whatever it is you're here for.

But unlike regular vehicles (aka cars!) you don't get to trade it in. So the sooner you can **fall in love** with your beautiful body and nourish it, care for it and respect it, the more magical and shiny your life will be.

Trust me. :)

★ #Girlboss of your bod

So, first things first. This is **your** body. You are the boss of it! That means you get to control who touches it, what food goes into it, how it moves, how you love/hate it, and the adventures you take it on. It's all you.

I remember doing a personal development course at about the age of sixteen. The teacher, who I'll admit I was a little bit scared of, said to us, 'You have to learn to love your body. What you don't love, change. And if you can't change it, learn to live with it because it ain't going anywhere!' She would say that if you don't like your nose, then either go get plastic surgery or learn to love it—those are your only two options. I loved her 'get over it' attitude. It woke me up and made me realise that we do have that choice.

I personally would say that you actually only have **one** option though, and that is to love it. Plastic surgery is not for young girls who are sad about their nose or boobs. It's for real life problems: a new breast because you've had to have one removed because of breast cancer; a new nose because you've had an accident and need to have it rebuilt in order to survive. That's where plastic surgery is truly magical. But to have it just because you would like to look like [insert latest celebrity bae here] is cowardly, dangerous and happening far too often if you ask me. #endofrant!

IRL ➜ My friend wants to get plastic surgery . . .

Seriously though, if you've got a friend telling you she's going to get a boob job as soon as she graduates, do what you can to talk some sense into her. Tell her all the things you love about her already. Remind her that we all have days when we don't love something about ourselves but that it's our duty to be great role models for younger girls and show them that the way we look isn't the most important thing in life. Be that shining light for someone else and help them see sense.

★ #Bodygoalz

So many people obsess over their looks. Have you noticed? How does it make you feel? Do you find yourself obsessing too? It's hard not to end up getting anxious or worried about how you look sometimes. Magazines and TV ads are always telling us to get, 'beach ready for summer' or putting highly-edited pictures of girls in our faces telling us to buy whatever they're selling in order to feel beautiful.

And I get it. Whether we like it or not, the way we look is a big part of who we are. Whether we like or dislike the way we look has a big impact on how we feel about ourselves. But the definition of what is beautiful in society is always changing. Being super focused on keeping up with what's beautiful (whether that's a bubble butt or being stick-thin) is exhausting and impossible. However, we can **embrace the parts of us that we love**.

Positive body image is how you feel about the way you look. It's not about how you look but **how you feel** about the way you look. Anyone can have positive body image, regardless of how they look.

> *Try This!* ➜ Remember being a kid, around three to five years old? If you ask kids that age what they love about their bodies, they say things like 'I love my hands because they can draw' and 'I love my legs because I can dance.' One three year old just said she loved everything! Let's remember what our bodies can **do** for us. And if you have a little one in your life, ask them!

The million dollar question is: *Why are we so hard on ourselves about the way we look?*

⭑ It's all art: magazines + social media

Ever looked at perfect images on social media accounts or in magazines and thought: 'That person has a perfect life; they are happy and I wish I was like that.' It's exactly what advertisers, influencers and marketing professionals want us to think. That's why we buy their stuff. We get sucked in because we want to feel the way **we think** that person feels. And right in front of us is a magical solution (like a protein bar or a skincare brand) that will help us get there.

Experts have found that looking at magazines for just sixty minutes lowers the self-esteem of over 80% of girls![7]

Have you ever been to a photoshoot? Looking at my old modelling photos, I can tell you that I **wish** I looked like those images of myself IRL. But I don't look like those images of myself! Each shoot takes hours of hair and make-up, perfect lighting (which always seems to take hours to get perfect), a professional photographer with years of experience, a stylist and experience in knowing how to pose a bunch of different ways. Plus hours of post-production work, where they will sometimes even change the structure of your body and face, remove any blemishes (pimples gone!), make things bigger and smaller (hello boobs that don't exist!) and basically turn you into an unrealistic human! #HELPimanalien

And that goes for social media too. Those 'fitspo' models, who make a living from having a big following, spend hours each day in the gym obsessing over the way they look (because this is their job after all); apply all sorts of tanning lotions and oils; take another hour or so to apply the perfect make-up; and then pose in a particular way to make their body appear how they want it to appear. And that's before they even take the photo (or hundreds). Not to mention the editing and filters applied after that. And the reason why they do all that? Because a protein

---

7   Dr. Raj Persuad, psychiatrist at Maudsley Hospital London. Cited in the Self Esteem Discussion Guide for Mothers and Daughters by The Dove Self-Esteem Fund Self http://www.wales.nhs.uk/sitesplus/documents/866/Activity%20Guide%20for%20 Mothers%20Daughters%2011–16yrs.pdf

powder or activewear company is paying them anywhere from $600+ a post to mention their product. It's all advertising, even when it doesn't seem like it.

If you're comparing yourself to an image you see in an advertisement, a movie star or even someone on social media, you may as well compare yourself to a beautiful painting or cartoon. Because that's how real it is.

We can't ignore all of these images in our lives but we can **appreciate them as art** rather than real life.

One thing I loved about modelling was being part of bringing a creative vision to life. Months go into creating a campaign, with art directors and designers working together to decide on the concept. They then find the perfect team to bring that vision to life, including the photographer, hair and make-up team, models, styling and location. It's pretty amazing to see it all come to life. **But it's not real**. It's art, baby.

★ Take shine-worthy action

Take notice of how you feel when you see images of other people now. See if you can appreciate them as art, instead of comparing yourself to them.

★ Lead a 'love your body' revolution!

Fat talk is an epidemic. You know what I'm talking about. Most girls I've chatted with seem to have at least one friend who does the whole, 'Ohhh, I look so fat in this. I'm so ugly. Blah blah blah.' You might respond with, 'Oh no, you are beautiful,' or 'Oh no, I'm fatter and uglier than you.' It's called 'fat talk' and **it has to stop**!

One of our recent students said she tackled her friend to the ground the other day when she started her usual fat talk.

This student was so upset because her friend is **beautiful**. First of all, it makes her feel crap about herself when her beautiful friend says she's ugly. Secondly, it's just not true and she knows this friend does it to get attention. So she tackled her to the ground and said she wouldn't let her get up until she admitted that she's beautiful. Maybe don't tackle, but I love how passionate she was about making sure her friend put an instant stop to that fat talk.

★ Take shine-worthy action

How can you do this too? #minusthetackle

It starts with you! **Be a leader** in your friendship group and make sure that girls everywhere grow up loving themselves and their bodies. If we don't stand up now, together, and put a stop to it, then our younger sisters will grow up hating on themselves even more. Lead the 'love your body' revolution in your own way.

★ You're in charge of what goes in

As the new head boss lady of your bod, you are in charge of what goes in. The food you eat, the products you slather onto your skin, what you drink—they are all choices that you make. Start making **conscious choices**.

Did you know? ➤ If you've been paying attention in biology, you'll probably know that we're all born with a sequence of DNA that doesn't change. But the cool thing is, our experiences and the way we live our life can change the way it is packaged and expressed. In fact, only around 25% of the variation in human longevity (how long you live for) is due to genetic factors[8]. The environment we create for ourselves has a bigger impact on how long we live! (So no blaming your parents for bad genes – ha!) Environmental factors such as food, drugs, or exposure to toxins can cause epigenetic changes[9], turning genes on or off or altering the way molecules bind to DNA. Even the social environments we inhabit can have an impact on how our DNA is expressed.[10] Enough science talk? All this means is, while some diseases and health conditions are a part of your make up, you actually have loads of control over how healthy your body is.

★ Food feelz

I want to make this section as simple as possible, because there is so much information on 'the Google' and it can get really complicated trying to figure out what's right and what's wrong. The thing is, there is no 'right' and 'wrong.' There is just food and your body and how you feel when they come together in a glorious mess of yumminess.

Let's keep it simple!

---

8   Passarino, G., De Rango, F., & Montesanto, A. (2016). Human longevity: Genetics or Lifestyle? It takes two to tango. *Immunity & Ageing : I & A, 13*, 12. http://doi.org/10.1186/s12979-016-0066-z

9   Gregory, S. Associate Professor of Medical Genetics. Source: http://dukemagazine.duke.edu/article/big-question-can-your-environment-change-your-dna

10 Slavich, G.M., & Cole, S.W. (2013). The Emerging Field of Human Social Genomics. *Clinical Psychological Science* DOI: 10.1177/2167702613478594

✓ Eat foods that make you **feel good long term** (not just for a taste explosion in your mouth that then makes you feel like sleeping for four hours—not so productive!) Start noticing how foods actually make you feel.

✓ Try to eat foods that are actually **real, living foods.** Next time you're at the supermarket, take notice of what's on the shelves. There's usually the section with the real, living food—fruits and vegetables that still resemble their original state. And then there are the aisles full of boxes, cans, bottles and packets of stuff that may have been food once, but have had so much stuff done to them to make sure they last on a shelf for years that they usually don't have many nutrients left. We want foods that give us **life**, not foods that died years ago and are pretending to be food. Like a box of cereal that includes dried strawberries—just get fresh strawberries!

✓ **Consider your values** when you think about the food you eat. For example, I'm vegan. I love animals and don't want to eat them. It seems strange to me to drink the breast milk of a cow when I'm not a baby cow. So I don't. That works for me and feels good. Figure out what works for your body and feels good for you.

✓ If you feel like you need more energy, want to sleep better, have better clarity and want to feel less anxious, then consider eating **more fresh vegetables, fruits, nuts and seeds.** The more you eat of the good stuff, the more you'll feel great and the less you'll turn to the aisles full of junk. It makes me sad to hear students talk about their anxiety in one breath and then about how they drink three diet sodas every day in the next breath. These things are related!!!

✓ **Don't restrict your intake** of food, like ever. Avoid anything that says 'diet.' They don't work (seriously, none of them work). Just eat healthier foods and you'll naturally crowd out the ones that don't make you feel great.

- ✓ And while you're avoiding the word 'diet,' don't be fooled by diet soft drinks or foods. **They are usually worse** than the sugar-filled ones. There's an ingredient in diet soft drinks called aspartame, which has been linked to all sorts of side effects, from headaches to depression to death!
- ✓ **Don't stress too much.** Getting obsessive over food, even healthy food, can lead to mental health issues. So eat healthy as much as you can and do it because you feel good when you eat that way. If you're busy and want to get on with life, you'll get much more done if you're fuelled properly! But when you feel like a big tub of ice cream, well go and enjoy it, baby! Maybe just look for a coconut ice cream instead of dairy and give it a try. See the 'swapsie-doodle' chapter coming up for ideas.
- ✓ **Try new things.** We can get so stuck in our own food ruts . . . like only eating hot chips when we go out for dinner. (Ahem, I'm talking to you little sister!) If you don't like something you can always spit it out, you won't die. And you might find a whole bunch of new foods that you love.
- ✓ **Do your own research** when it interests you. If someone says, 'eating apples will kill you,' maybe look that up for yourself and see what you find. Use your common sense.
- ✓ **Remember the whole picture.** Health and wellness isn't just about weight, shape or looks. It's about feeling good and getting active so you can make the most of every day, concentrate when you need to and be **full of life.**

★ Take shine-worthy action

Take notice of how you feel next time you're eating:

- Are there particular foods that make you feel bloated?
- Are there particular foods that give you long-lasting energy?

We're all different, so what feels right for you will be different to what feels right for others. Let's release judgement and tune into what suits us.

★ Eat with the seasons

Beautiful Mama Earth provides so much goodness for us. But some crops can only grow at certain times of the year, like mangoes and cherries in summertime. And even though you can buy apples every day of the year, they can only be picked for a few months of the year. The rest of the time they can be stored in special conditions, to make sure they don't ripen fully. Bananas, which are also usually picked before they ripen so they are easy to transport, can be sprayed with a special hormone to turn them yellow before hitting the supermarket shelves. So rather than eating a ten-month-old apple, find out when fruits and vegetables ripen in your area. Or better still, go to a local farmers' market, find an organic stall and buy from them—whatever they have will be in season. When foods are in season, it's usually the best time for us to eat them too.

Some foods that are really good for us actually look like parts of our body! Ahhh, nature is amazing! For example:

- Kidney beans are great for our kidneys.
- Sliced carrots look similar to our eyes and are great for our eyesight.
- Avocadoes take nine months to ripen (just like a baby!) and look a bit like a womb. And wouldn't you know, they target the health and function of the womb and cervix. They help women balance hormones and deter cervical cancers. Plus, they are great for our skin (an added bonus).

- Walnuts, which look like the brain, are great for our brain function.
- Celery, which kind of looks like a bone, is great for our bones.

Fascinating, right?

★ Be a hero for Mama Earth

I know you're a kind soul and are so much more aware of what's going on in the world than us oldies. You know about global warming, you know that there is hunger all over the world, and you do really 'get' how lucky we are to be born at a time when things are a-changing. I know you want to make a difference in this world.

And I know you're keen to learn more about choosing foods with minimal impact on Mama Earth.

Food mileage

Some food comes from the other side of the planet. Can you imagine how much goes into getting it to your plate? The travel, the chemicals that might be sprayed to make sure it doesn't get eaten by bugs on the way, the people who had to harvest it and move it and the fuel that was used on the journey . . . it all has an impact on the planet. So next time you're shopping for food, check where things come from. See if you can find foods that are made or grown locally. This will support your local farmers and keep the 'food mileage' down. #goodkarma

Food wastage

Tons of food gets thrown away each year. Do what you can to reduce this. Here are some ideas to get you started:

- Don't put too much on your plate in the first place. If you want more, go back for seconds!
- Make sure you have a compost bin or see if you can find a local community garden where you can drop off food waste, so that it goes back to the earth to support growing more food.

We recently moved from acreage, where we had our own veggie garden, into a tiny apartment in the city. But that hasn't stopped us. There is a community garden around the corner and our unit complex even has its own worm farm and herb garden!

Ethics with food

Research what actually happens to your food. Do you know how a lamb roast gets to your plate? How do you feel about that? Do you know how the people who harvested your coffee beans are treated? It's impossible to know it all, but we can **start to be aware** and start asking questions.

To be a good custodian of Mama Earth, try to:

- Support local businesses and farms as much as possible.
- Eat less animal products. In 2006 the United Nations Food and Agricultural Organisation reported[11] that animals raised for food (the livestock sector) generate more greenhouse gas emissions (18% as measured on CO_2 equivalent) than transport! Livestock also generates 65% of human-related nitrous oxide (mostly from the animals' poo!), which has 296 times the Global Warming Potential of CO_2. It's also a major source of land and water degradation. So, it helps Mama Earth (and the animals) to eat less meat.
- Go organic.

11 Steinfeld, Henning. 2006. *Livestock's long shadow: environmental issues and options.* Rome: Food and Agriculture Organization of the United Nations.

- Look out for 'fair trade' labels on things like coffee and chocolate, which often come from third world countries. If it's fair trade, it means the workers have been paid a fair wage and the companies aren't using slave or child labour.

Try this! ➤ It's all energy . . .

When we eat something, it turns into energy in our bodies. It's like that energy is transferred from the food, to us. Everything has an energy and, if you imagine picking an apple straight off the tree (because I seem to be obsessed with apples in this book), it's going to be alive with nutrients and energy from the mama tree! When I'm eating something, I like to imagine that energy is moving from the food into my body and I try to remember to feel grateful for this. Even if it's a plant and not an animal, it's still being sacrificed, in a way, for me to eat it.

Next time you eat, try to imagine that energy and feel grateful to the food, the people who brought it to you and mama earth for providing it. Or disregard this paragraph as crazy-talk if you like, I won't be offended!

★ Take shine-worthy action

- Start helping out in the kitchen. The more you can get into the kitchen and learn your way around it, the better. And Mum, Dad or whoever prepares the meals in your household will love you for it. Get in there, help them chop food and ask what else you can do to be useful. Eventually you will start to feel comfortable in there by yourself and you can start to experiment. Maybe start by making your own lunches, so you can begin to take more responsibility for your health.

- Make food shopping fun! Go with your parents (or whoever shops) next time and take notice of all the stuff on the shelves. Find out where things come from, look at the ingredients and make sure you know what you're eating. There's are apps you can download to figure out what particular numbers and other chemicals are in the ingredients list (though I try to avoid numbers and big words I don't understand!).

★ Eat like a monk: mindful eating

Ever eat in front of the TV? Or check your phone nonstop throughout your meal? When we do this, it's easy to eat an entire meal without tasting it, or even noticing it. And then we eat more and more, because we are not tuned in to how our body is feeling and really being present while eating.

Top tips for mindful eating:

1. Sit down! Even if it's only for ten minutes, make time to actually sit and enjoy your meal.
2. Switch off the TV, laptop, phone and focus on the food. Who knows, you might have a nice conversation with your family or friends if you are sitting down and enjoying a meal together.
3. Turn on your senses. Really enjoy and take notice of the taste, smell and texture of each bite.
4. Chew it baby! Digestion starts in your mouth (not your stomach) so chewing properly allows the saliva to do its work and makes life easier for your stomach. It can also take our brains some time to get the signal that we are full. So slow down. Around 30 times per mouthful is the going rate

if you can do it! More for something tough like a brazil nut. How many times do you chew each bite?

5. Observe your body. Notice if your tummy is rumbling or if you are feeling tired. Tune in and consciously feed your body energy with each yummy bite of food.

✦ Foods with superpower

Incorporate some super-duper foods into your day for an instant boost! Superfoods are nutritionally rich foods that offer tremendous dietary and healing potential. Why do we need them? Because these days even our regular fruits and vegetables aren't what they used to be. Our soils are depleted of nutrients; many fruits and vegetables have been sprayed with chemicals (unless organic); and as I mentioned earlier, our supermarkets are full of packaged and processed foods.

We are also surrounded by environmental pollutants on a daily basis—from car fumes, beauty products and household cleaning products to being permanently attached to technology. So wherever we can get an extra little boost, the better!

> *It is becoming clearer that to achieve the best health ever, the best relationship with food ever, and the most fun with our food ever, we must consume super-foods, superherbs, and raw living food cuisine.*
>
> David Wolfe, author and raw food guru

Cacao

This raw, unprocessed form of chocolate can come as cacao beans, cacao powder and cacao butter. A number one source of magnesium, it supports the heart, relaxes menstrual cramps, builds strong bones and increases alkalinity (our bodies thrive best in an alkaline environment). It's also rich in serotonin, which helps to build up our 'stress defence shield.'

Goji berries

These little red dried berries boost immune function, increase alkalinity, provide liver protection and improve eyesight and blood quality.

Spirulina

This algae from the ocean is usually found in powder form and has the highest concentration of protein found in any food. It's also a complete protein (containing as much iron as red meat), is high in antioxidants and boosts the immune system.

Chia seeds

Chia seeds soak up liquid, making them perfect for puddings and jelly-like desserts. They deliver massive amounts of nutrients with very few calories and contain a very high amount of antioxidants. They can also improve exercise performance.

Note: These super foods sometimes come from the other side of the planet, depending on where you live. So where possible, buy locally-produced options and if you can't find local variations, buy them sparingly and treat them with lots of respect. They've come so far to serve you!

★ Swapsie-doodles

There is a healthy and live alternative to most of our favourite foods, so it can be fun to play swapsie-doodles and try some of these:

Milk chocolate	Raw organic cacao or dark chocolate
Cheese	Raw cheeses made from nuts
Sugar	Natural sweeteners such as stevia, dates, coconut sugar, brown rice syrup
Ice cream	Coconut ice cream or make some banana nice cream (freeze chopped up bananas, then thaw slightly and throw into a blender. Delish!)
Pasta	Zucchini spirals (you can make these with a spiralizer or you can even use a vegetable peeler to create zucchini fettucine) or organic, gluten-free pasta, if you're allergic to gluten
White rice	Brown rice or quinoa (cooks like rice and is light and fluffy, but is high in protein and is actually a seed rather than a grain!)
Cow's milk	Homemade almond mylk (super easy to make!)
Anything in a box, can, jar or packet	The fresh, live version of it, eg. instead of a tin of tomatoes, use fresh ones.
Coffee or black tea	Herbal teas (many different varieties which all taste different and help you feel different things, eg. I'm drinking 'tulsi' tea which is helping me focus right now.)
Soft drinks or energy drinks	Anything else! They are bad, man. Drink more water and find a way to make it nice for yourself, because it helps you with so many things—your skin, sleep, stress, bowel movements, exercise. Your body is 80% water, so drink up! Add lemon or raspberries, a sprig of mint or make it sparkling if it helps you drink it.

★ Don't poison yourself

I'm a bit of a weirdo—I don't drink alcohol. Students always find that strange when I tell them, because it's such a huge part of society. So many people socialise around alcohol. I chose to stop drinking when I was diagnosed with cancer. It seemed plain stupid to me to put poison in my body when it's such a beautiful gift. When I had so much poison being pumped into my body already to try to get well with chemotherapy, it just didn't feel right to bring alcohol back into my life.

It's no big deal. I just drink a juice or sparkling water when I'm out and about with friends. I catch up for tea, coffee, yummy food, walks in the park, swims at the beach—fun stuff that doesn't involve getting trashed and doing something I'll regret the next day.

I spent too much time in my early twenties partying. I can't believe I managed to come out the other side to be honest. I know so many people who are messed up now because of the choices they made in their teens or early twenties.

Don't do something just because someone else is doing it. You're stronger than that.

It's an addiction. I believe that if alcohol and cigarettes didn't make so much money for governments, then they would be banned. It always starts with 'just a little bit' and can seem harmless but it changes the atmosphere of an environment, it stops people thinking clearly and increases crime, violence and a whole host of bad choices.

By the way, I don't judge others—they can do what they like. I know lots of lovely, smart people who do drink alcohol. I just choose not to do it myself.

One more thing on this . . . if you're going to try something, make sure you tell your parents, are with friends who love you and make sure you have one sober driver who's looking out for you. #endofmotherlyspeech

THE POWER OF YOUR CYCLE

★ Power within

Imagine if you could map out your whole month . . . Knowing when you're going to feel a little more sluggish and tired and knowing when you're going to be **full** of energy. Knowing when you can be the most productive. Knowing when you want to be around people, can even get a little flirty (oh my!) and feel your most confident. Well you can, and it all lies within understanding your cycle.

> *As a woman you are coded for power, and the journey to realising the fullness and beauty of that power—your Wild Power—lies in the rhythm and change of your menstrual cycle.*
>
> **Alexandra Pope and Sjanie Hugo Wurlitzer in the book *Wild Power***

It's time ladies, we're talking about periods . . .
'Eerrgghhh! I've got my period.'
'Aunt Flow has come to visit.'
'Got my rags.'
'It's shark week.'

'That time of the month again.'

'Are you on your period again or something? Is that why you're cranky?'

This monthly ritual that almost all women experience is a beautiful gift and a **huge** part of our life. But we often sweep it under the carpet, pretend it doesn't exist and would **never** talk about it openly. So embarrassing!

When you're trying to get out of class so you can rush to the bathroom and check if you've got your period, it's easy to forget that this whole cycle occurs to bring beautiful babies into the world. Our wombs get ready for a baby to settle in there each month, just in case, and if a baby doesn't come, the lining gets washed away (our periods) ready to start the process again.

But it's so much more than just a baby-making function of our body.

Did you know? ➤ The average Western woman will have her period for 6½ to 7 years of her life! That's a big chunk of our lives! So let's learn a little more about it and how you can make this a really positive experience for you.

★ Learning about this magical part of being a woman

We're all so different and experience our cycle in different ways. Some girls do seem to feel more pain and may need extra support from a naturopath or doctor to figure out what's going on, while some girls don't feel any. Some get their periods like clockwork every month and some are quite irregular. We're all different, so it's important to tune into how you can work best with your own cycle and ask for help if something doesn't feel right for you or you're in pain.

How you nourish your body and rest throughout your cycle can have a big impact on whether you feel pain or not during your period. For example, reducing sugar and dairy throughout the cycle, and particularly in the lead-up to your period, has been shown to reduce pain.

Something I wish I knew right from the start is you can chart your cycle and do your best to live in harmony with it. For example, you might notice that you're very motivated at a certain time of the month and so you can make sure you sit down and smash out lots of your assessment during this time. That way when you're not feeling up to it later in the cycle, you can go to bed early with a hot water bottle and watch your favourite show, without feeling like you're getting behind.

The tools

These days you can now find organic cotton pads, panty liners and tampons. You can even find reusable products which save on wastage, like cloth pads. You might not feel comfortable with these at school, but you could wear a reusable cloth pad at home when you go to sleep at night, wash it in the morning and wear something disposable during the day at school. Do some research about them—there are loads of different brands of cloth pads now and even some that are sewn into underwear. So easy!

There are these amazing menstrual cups that you can get now too! I'll let you do your research on these as well but they're a great way to reduce waste, as you just buy one or two of them. Most girls I know who use a menstrual cup only need to change it once or twice during a day, so they're really convenient.

Have a little purse that you always carry with you containing sanitary products (tampons and liners), a bottle of essential oil or a spritzer designed to balance your hormones and a clean pair of underwear just in case. This will be great for you but also for your girlfriends. How amazing if you could be the person who saves the day when your friend gets her period all of a sudden at school? #periodhero

In the book *A Blessing Not a Curse*, Jane Bennett suggests finding out what the school policy is. Do you know where to go, if you do get your period at school? Does the school nurse have some supplies to help you out? It's good to know, just in case. If you don't want to ask, ask your parents to find out for you.

And **celebrate** it! Since having chemotherapy, I no longer get my period and have been advised that I've gone into early menopause. When I was younger I would have been happy about this but I now realise just how magical it can be. It's a symbol of hope, health and abundance. It's a reminder that everything is a cycle and things sometimes feel good and bad but they always come back around. And of course, without it you can't have children and your body starts to go into 'old age' mode (early menopause means things like brittle bones, older-looking skin, etc.).

So please celebrate it when it comes, make an event of it, chat with your girlfriends about it and watch each other's back, literally!

★ What actually happens?

We asked our trusty naturopath (Kasey Willson) about this, to find out exactly what's going on inside the body.

Your menstrual cycle begins at puberty, with an initial surge of oestrogen from your ovaries, stimulated by the pituitary gland in your brain. This oestrogen promotes the growth of your breasts, the development of your reproductive system and the shape of your body (you might start filling out around the hips, for example). Cycles are often irregular for a year after your initial period, as the body find its natural cycle and your first period is often very light.

Although it can change from cycle to cycle and from one woman to the next, a textbook cycle will last for 28 days and the average cycle is 29½ days, which is the same as the moon cycle. How cool is that? Everything in nature is so beautifully connected. The cycle can go from 24-35 days, though everyone is a little different.

Day one of your cycle is the first day of your period (not including spotting) and the last day of your cycle is the day before menstrual bleeding begins once again.

The words:

- Menarche—your first period (welcome to womanhood, a time to celebrate!)
- Menstruation—the technical word for your period, usually lasts from three to seven days.
- Menopause—when your period stops (usually in older women, unless there are health issues).
- Ovaries—the home of all of our eggs. We have two ovaries, about the size of an almond in the shell.
- Menstrual cycle—goes from menstruation (your period) to ovulation, back to menstruation. The menstrual cycle is actually triggered in the brain which sends a message to the reproductive system to signal the start of the cycle.
- Ovulation—when the egg is ripening and forms a little cyst on the wall of your ovary.

Extra info! ➤ The magical menstrual cycle is nothing to be embarrassed or ashamed about. But it can take a bit of getting used to. I know lots of women in their thirties and forties who are at last starting to work with their cycles, rather than being annoyed at the 'nuisance' of them.

Don't have your period yet? You can start to track your own inner cycle, by getting in tune with the moon cycle instead. Look it up (and look up!) and start noticing how you feel on the new moon, full moon, etc.

★ Living in tune with your cycle

Yep, we're still talking about periods. Stay with me here . . . this is powerful information! No-one's looking over your shoulder at what's on the page in front of you. You're safe.

A really cool way to look at the menstrual cycle is by aligning each stage with the seasons—winter, spring, summer and autumn.

Winter is when we're menstruating (or have our period and are actually bleeding). We usually feel more like hibernating, hanging out at home in bed with a block of chocolate, generally happy to have a bit more quiet time away from others.

Spring is what comes next, once our period is finished. We feel lighter, have new energy, enthusiasm and can think clearly. So if you've got a problem that you can't quite figure out, you might decide to wait until this time to revisit it, then find that it's much easier to make sense of and come to a decision. We can be more creative during this time too. This is when egg development is occurring.

Summer is ovulation time. This is the magical time when the fully-matured follicle has made its way to the surface of the ovary and ejects an egg into your abdominal cavity. During this time, your body is at the optimum state to get pregnant. Your body is ready and so you usually feel more sparkly and more social. You want to get 'out there' more. This is a great time to schedule catch-ups with friends or an audition or job interview.

Autumn is the time we're winding down to menstruation and about to get our period. A different hormone called progesterone is more dominant in the second half of the cycle and, just like in the garden in autumn, you may feel like pruning and winding down to winter again. It's a great time to declutter, clean up your bedroom and sort things out. Cool, huh?

As women, it's important to acknowledge that each stage is valuable and to support ourselves when we're not quite as 'summery' as we would like to be **all the time**.

Once your cycle is pretty regular, you might like to chat with your family (or at least the women in the household) about how you can manage it together. For instance, letting them know when it's nearly time for you to get your period, so that everyone gives you a little more space. And at the same time, understanding where your mum and any other girls in your household are in their cycle, so that you can help each other out and support one another.

★ Menstrual wellness

You can even create some simple rituals that you do each month as you get your period. For example:

- Have a bath when you get your period with some beautiful, calming essential oils and some Epsom salts.
- Buy or pick yourself flowers.
- Drink herbal teas (try to stay away from coffee and caffeinated teas—go for relaxing blends like chamomile).

- Paint your nails.
- Watch trashy TV or read a book.
- Meditate. It's been said that we're more connected to our spirit during this time and are naturally more quiet in the mind. It's a great time to practise meditation and get quiet within.
- Some yoga poses are great to relieve any discomfort during your period. Do a bit of a search online to find videos you can watch. We've listed some on our website too.
- Buy yourself some good-quality dark chocolate or even make yourself a hot chocolate with cacao. We often crave chocolate during our period and that's because the good-quality stuff (not the milk chocolate that's usually full of sugar!) is high in magnesium, which helps our muscles to relax. This can ease cramps.
- Come up with some rituals together with your mum or girl-friends if you like.

Give yourself permission to be slower, gentler and more introverted when your period is coming. This is the time to say 'no' if you feel like it. Going shopping, for example, probably won't feel as fun when you have your period, as you'll naturally be feeling heavier, slower and a little rounder.

A friend of mine used to have quite intense period pain but she's recently realised that if she just stays in bed for the first day of her period, not even working on her laptop but just relaxing, she doesn't feel pain at all. Sometimes our body is just telling us we need to be more gentle.

Feeling pain with your period? A bit of discomfort is common: aching down the legs, nausea, headaches, loose bowels can all be experienced during this time of the month. But if you're in pain, you should see a doctor.

★ Take shine-worthy action

When you have your period, keep a diary for the next month to see how you feel each day. You can even download an app to do this—there are heaps around. Take notice of when you feel like summer, spring, winter and autumn, so you can start to plan out your months.

SLEEP, YOGA + MOVING YOUR TOOSH

Consider this. We were never designed to:

- sit at desks and computers, detached from our bodies all day
- be scrunched into cars for our daily commute or go all day without walking more than a few hundred metres
- spend hours on the couch
- be so detached from the seasons that we barely notice winter is over until spring sales begin
- consume so much of other peoples' lives and experiences via social media that we totally miss the beauty, majesty and uniqueness of our own life
- be regimented in an artificial timetable of to-do lists, appointments and work hours, where taking a moment to hear ourselves is drowned out by traffic, earphones and radio stations!

We should be free and out in nature! So we have to work on tuning out all the noise and tuning in to our own gut instincts, feelings and thoughts. We have to consciously **find the calm.**

★ Just breathe

We spend our lives breathing, without ever having to think about it. But when we do tune into our breath and take notice of it, we instantly feel more calm. So I'd love you to stop for a moment and take one, deep, slow breath through your nose and down into your belly. Then exhale as slowly as you can, out through your nose. Repeat a few times. You'll notice that you can go a little deeper each time and you might even notice that your belly rises a little. Your heart rate might slow down and you'll feel more present in your body.

This is something you can do anytime, especially when you're feeling stressed out or worried about something. You can do it in the classroom, on the bus or lying in bed. Just breathe.

If you feel like you need something else to distract you, look at a watch or clock and count five seconds in and five seconds out with your breathing. Simple but **powerful**.

★ Sleep

Teens need at least nine hours sleep a night. But it takes more than your head hitting the pillow to have a good night's sleep. You should wake feeling refreshed and ready for the day. How do you feel when you wake in the morning?

Megan Dalla-Camina, author of *Getting Real About Having It All,* says:

> *Sleep deprivation can cause a lack of motivation, moodiness, inability to cope with stress, reduced immunity, lack of concentration and memory problems, increased risk of accidents, major health problems like heart disease and, wait for it ladies—weight gain.*

Here are some tips to get a good night's sleep:

- Make sure your room is dark.
- Turn off all electronic devices in your room—even the TV's standby light can inhibit sleep.
- Make sure your **phone is off** or at the very least on flight mode.
- Get off your phone, computer and any other magical device an hour before bedtime. This is crucial. Read a book (non-school related, so your brain can start to wind down), do some stretches, have a cup of restful herbal tea or journal instead.

★ *#Yogaeverydamnday*

Amongst the stress that is placed on teenage girls, we often forget how important self-care and love is. It feels as though there are not enough hours in the day to complete the tasks required of us (study, exercise, socialising, sleep, work, family time, etc.) and we get overwhelmed and caught up. By simply spending a few minutes a day to relax, meditate, stretch, do yoga (I do three sun salutations) you can re-centre yourself and feel instantly calmer, thus working and just living in general more effectively and efficiently.

Ruby 17, past student, sharing what works for her

You might not be into yoga or you might not have tried it. That's okay. But find **something** that you like to do to move your body. Not being into sports is kind of a cop-out these days, when you have so many more options than just joining the local netball team.

I've met plenty of girls who give themselves the label 'not sporty' and don't do anything to move their body. This will cause all sorts of problems later in life and will also be affecting your day-to-day life right now.

Exercising regularly helps us to:

- sleep properly at night
- sweat out toxins and detox the body
- feel good, as it releases feel-good hormones that literally make us happier
- reduce stress and can be a great way to get out a bunch of feelings (Feeling angry at your little brother? Go for a run or to a boxing class and watch the anger fade away!)
- be more productive

So don't use 'too much homework' as an excuse for not moving your toosh. Put down the books and go for a walk—you'll come back fresher, with new ideas and ready to keep going. The trick is finding something you actually want to do. So start exploring.

Here are some ideas to get you started:

- ✓ Try a dance class—Zumba, Latin, contemporary, hip-hop—find something that sounds fun to you and join up! Sometimes adult classes are the best because they're full of women like me, who have two left feet and are just doing it for fun. That will take the pressure off.
- ✓ Try a few different yoga classes. Yoga can be so different— gentle and slow or powerful and strong. Some classes are in 40° heat and the instructor pretty much yells at you, other classes are spent pretty much sleeping for half the class. There's even aerial yoga where you hang upside down—so fun! Find what you love and commit to going each week.
- ✓ Grab a friend and commit to doing something together.

✓ Walk the dog. But not like once in a blue moon. Commit to doing it a few times a week and challenge yourself—walk further or find hills so it's more than just a stroll.

✓ Download an app—a yoga one with a few poses to do at home just before bed, or a fitness one that takes you through a bunch of squats and sit-ups to do for half an hour before school. You can find a list of our favourites at shinefromwithinhq.com

✓ Join a sporting team.

SELF-CARE RITUALS

~

We touched on the importance of creating rituals for ourselves under Menstrual Wellness (Page 100) but let's expand for a moment here.

I know your life is super busy. That's why rituals are so great. They become little habits that you do each day, week or month to give back to **you** so you can keep on going. While you're still at school and in a constant cycle of to-do lists, classes and activities, this is actually the perfect time to add some of your own beautiful rituals to your life.

What makes a self-care ritual?

1. It makes you feel good **and** restores you. (So maybe not a regular ice cream binge—you would probably feel pretty gross afterwards, even if your tastebuds loved it at the time!)
2. It occurs regularly. (So not like a one-off massage once a year.)

Self-care rituals don't have to be complicated or fancy. In fact, the simpler the better. You probably already have a bunch of self-care rituals in place, you just don't realise it.

Some ideas include:

- Journalling each evening as you lie in bed getting ready for sleep. Get a notebook and just write what comes into your head. It doesn't have to make sense, it can just help to get thoughts down on paper.
- Going to netball each week. If this makes you happy and gets your body moving, then that's a self-care ritual.
- Stretching in the morning before you get ready for school.
- Putting your rollerskates on, a sweatband around your forehead, some high socks, knee pads and fluoro activewear, then rollerskating down the street. (Hey, whatever floats your boat!)
- Cleansing and moisturising your face each night.
- Having a bath once a week.
- Reading fantasy novels for half an hour before sleep.
- Putting on your favourite song while you're getting ready for school.
- Having a green smoothie each afternoon when you get home.
- Turning off your phone and computer at a certain time each night—this is a self-care ritual too.
- Watching a bit of TV after school. I know this can be frowned upon but honestly, just sitting there and tuning out for a while can actually be very restorative and help you calm down after a full-on day. (Just don't get stuck in a six-hour binge session—trust me, you won't feel great after that!)
- Getting creative once a week or once a month with craft, art, gardening, jewellery making, candle making or a colouring-in book.

The key to a great self-care ritual is making sure it's scheduled in. Of course, there will be times when you're not able to do it. But if you get into a habit of doing it regularly and, most importantly, know you can do it when you are starting to feel extra stressed or not like your usual self, then it will be beneficial for you.

Take shine-worthy action

Create a self-care menu or list for yourself. Make it pretty and stick it on your wall. Do something from that list each day if you can, but don't feel bad if you don't get something done. The important thing here is that you do something on the list when you're feeling stressed, to bring peace back into your life.

Part 2
Shine on the outside

GLOWING SKIN

★ Al naturale

I had problem skin when I was in my late teens (yep, right around formal time, thanks!) and I would have done **anything** to make it go away. I got seduced by all the 'magical' formulas and products with celebrity faces on them, but nothing worked. I was very lucky that my beautiful mama took me to our family doctor then a dermatologist (skin specialist). I had chemical fruit peels, micro-dermabrasion and was put on the contraceptive pill. All of these things had long-term negative consequences and if I could go back in time, I wouldn't have done any of it. But we didn't know any better.

Now I do. So if you have problem skin, assess what's going on **inside** first. Our skin is usually a representation of what's going on inside our bodies, so things like hydration, diet, stress levels and hormones all play a part in the condition of our skin. Whether your skin is gorgeously glowing or you have some problems at the moment, here's what I wish I knew back then . . .

The key is to encourage and strengthen your skin's natural processes, rather than trying to 'strip' away oils or 'fix' your face with harsh chemicals.

What you need to know

Our skin is the largest organ of the body and helps it to eliminate toxins. So when the little holes on our skin (pores) are clogged because we don't take off our make-up or give our skin a good regular scrub, then we can get pimples or other skin conditions. These pores also absorb what we put on our skin; chemicals from lotions and perfume for example, all go straight into our bloodstream through the skin.

Straight to the bloodstream

Ever seen a TV ad for nicotine patches? They are applied to the skin and help smokers get their nicotine hit without actually smoking a cigarette. They work so effectively because the nicotine can be absorbed through the skin and go straight into the bloodstream. In fact, the skin absorbs up to 60-80% of the products we apply, so choosing natural products is really important.

Can you believe this?

There is no regulatory body that governs cosmetic products. According to the smart folks at the Environmental Working Group, out of 10,500 ingredients used today, 89% have not been evaluated for safety. This means that we have to be our own watchdogs and know exactly what we are putting onto our skin.

Read the label

Many beauty products now have one of the following words on their label: natural, organic, pure, botanical or plant-derived. But don't be fooled, these words don't mean much unless there is also some type of formal certification listed. It's important to look closely at the label and read the ingredients list. When reading a list of ingredients, the order is important: the first listed is the one featured most in the product, moving on down to what's featured least. So work your way down the ingredients list and, if you find a whole bunch of words you can't pronounce at the top of the list (or anywhere really), then beware!

For detailed information about specific products, their ingredients and the health problems that these ingredients have been linked to, visit the Environmental Working Group's 'Skin Deep Cosmetics Database.' They provide a score from 0-10 (with 0 being the least hazardous and 10 being the most hazardous), as well as a breakdown of each ingredient. http://www.cosmeticsdatabase.com

Did you know? ➤ Our skin is regenerated about every 28 days. So when trialling a new product, make sure you use it for at least that long before making a decision about it.

★ What's your skin type?

A great way to determine your skin type is to cleanse your skin with a gentle cream cleanser, then leave it bare for about half an hour.

Don't have a cream cleanser? Try a gentle fresh fruit face mask (like the one on Page 128 with banana and strawberries) and then rinse off and leave your skin bare for about half an hour.

Average/middle skin

Average/middle (normal) skin can be classified as having an even, smooth surface. It is neither oily or dry and will feel comfortable after doing this test. I don't like to call it 'normal' skin though, as that's suggesting that every other type is abnormal, which is not correct! We're all normal, we just all have different skin.

Oily skin

Oily skin can be classified as skin that has an over secretion of oil and is regularly oily and shiny. Generally the pores are larger and the excess oil can cause the skin to be more susceptible to blackheads and pimples. If your skin is shiny after the above test, then you probably have oily skin.

Dry skin

Dry skin can have a dull appearance and be flaky. Dry skin can often be sensitive, red and easily irritated, so requires a more nourishing moisturiser. If your skin feels tight or rough to touch after the above test, then you have dry skin.

Combination skin

Combination skin is usually oily in the T-Zone, which includes your forehead, nose and chin, and may be dry on the other parts of the face. If your skin is only shiny in the T-zone after the test, then you have combination skin.

Sensitive skin

Sensitive skin can be oily, normal or dry. What sets it apart is that it becomes red and irritated quite easily. This can be caused by the environment, skincare products or make-up. If you know you have sensitive skin, test products on the back of your hand before applying to your face.

What should I use?

Regardless of the type of skin you have (and they are **all** beautiful!), go for natural, preferably 'certified organic' skincare products that are vegan. They should feel gentle on your skin and not strip it of its natural oils.

Not sure if you should use a foaming face wash, facial wipes or a cream cleanser? There are so many different types of products on the market and it really comes down to what feels nice on your skin. Typically, if you have oily skin then you'll probably be more drawn to a light cleanser that is gel or water-based and foams a little. But if you have dry skin, you'll find that these products will dry your skin even more so will prefer the feel of an oil-based, nourishing cleanser. As long as it's natural and you've checked the ingredients, go for what feels nice on your skin.

Download a list of ingredients to avoid and look out for from our website: shinefromwithinhq.com

Extra info! ➤ Ever get puffy eyes?

If you have puffy eyes, place a slice of cold avocado, a slice of cucumber or a teabag (which has been soaked, wrung out and chilled) on each eye, to soothe and reduce the puffiness.

★ Skincare routine to shine

This is like a dance routine for your skin! Take the following three steps, every morning and night:

Step 1: Cleanse

Cleanse morning and evening—twice in the evening, if you are wearing make-up (coconut oil is the **best** way to remove eye make-up btw). To cleanse, dampen your face with warm water (to open the pores ready for cleaning), apply the cleanser to your fingertips and massage into your face, neck and décolletage in a circular motion (your décolletage is just below your neck, where your collarbone is). Gently remove with warm water and a face washer, by wringing out most of the water and then pressing the face washer onto your skin for a beautiful compress (don't wipe it aggressively).

Step 2: Tone

After cleansing, spritz the face with a refreshing toner to close the pores. You can also splash your face with cold water, which also closes your pores.

Step 3: Moisturise

Moisturising is essential morning and night, even if you have oily skin. Apply while your skin is still damp from the toner and gently massage into the face, neck and décolletage. This will nourish the skin and provide a protective film. Girls with oily skin or problem skin sometimes avoid moisturiser and try to dry their skin out as much as possible. However, this can cause the skin to produce even more oil! (Probably not what you're going for!)

Extra tips for your skincare routine

✓ **Exfoliate** twice a week. Exfoliating products are scrubs that have rough ingredients, to gently remove dead skin cells that can build up on the surface of skin and clog the pores (increasing the likelihood of pimples forming). But exfoliating more than twice a week is too harsh for the skin, so if you have a daily cleanser that feels rough, swap it for a gentler one. When purchasing a scrub, go for a natural brand. Some scrubs contain tiny round balls made of plastic, which cause lots of problems in the ocean—they wash down the sink and eventually out to sea. Poor fish!

✓ **Mask** once a week or once a fortnight. Face masks are a great way to provide a deeper cleanse or deeper nourishment for your skin. Clay masks are great for drawing out impurities and giving a deeper cleanse; moisturising masks will add an extra hit of nourishment to soften and smooth your skin. Don't forget to check out the face mask recipes starting on page 128.

Extra Info! ➤ Naturopath Kasey Willson's five ways to support skin heath:

1. **Hydrate.** Aim to drink 1.5–2 litres of filtered water a day. Add in extra liver detox support by squeezing the juice of ½ lemon into your morning glass of water. Kasey advises that 'fuelling your body with clean, filtered water is fundamental for healthy, glowing skin.'

2. **Move.** Getting a sweat up supports your lymph system, which takes nutrients to and waste from the cells of your body and is therefore crucial for clear skin.

3. **Poo like a champ!** For clear skin, it is important to have a well-functioning large intestine, so you can eliminate excess hormones and toxins from your body. Aim for one complete, well-formed bowel movement per day. (Google Bristol stool #4.) Filling up your meals and drinks with fresh vegetables, fruit, nuts and seeds provides the valuable

fibre to achieve this. By focusing on wholefoods, you are also crowding out those foods that upset gut health and often contribute to poor skin health. Such foods include unhealthy trans fats (found in heated and rancid seed oil: cottonseed oil, canola oil, soy bean oil, peanut oil, rice bran oil, corn oil, grapeseed oil, safflower oil, sunflower oil and vegetable oil) as well as sugar.

4. **Fermented Foods.** Try fermented foods such as sauerkraut, kim chi, coconut water kefir, kombucha and coconut yoghurt. These foods boost the good bacteria in your large intestine and play an essential role in supporting healthy elimination of toxins from your body. A healthy gut is known to support clear, glowing skin.

5. **Reduce Stress.** Stress can impact on your skin health by increasing stress hormones and encouraging sex hormone imbalances in your body. These imbalances can be a trigger for skin breakouts.

★ Help! I've got a pimple

You've heard it before: you shouldn't squeeze a pimple. And that's true. Squeezing a pimple can often spread the infection under the surface of the skin, which means you'll get an even bigger pimple tomorrow. However, **no-one** wants to leave the house with a giant whitehead on their face.

So if you do need to remove or reduce the size of a pimple, follow these simple instructions to do it in a way that will do the least amount of damage (less scarring, less redness and less chance of another big one appearing tomorrow!):

1. Fill a basin with warm water and add five drops of lavender or tea tree essential oil (if you have it, no big deal if you don't).
2. Ring out a face washer and press it against the zit–the heat will soften it and the lavender will help disinfect the area.
3. Get two tissues and wrap them around your fingertips. Press gently on the pimple, trying to get underneath the infected part. Hopefully it will all come out.
4. After you squeeze, dab on some of the tea tree or lavender oil and leave to dry.
5. If you have to cover it up, wait until it has dried and started to form a scab. Then gently dab a tiny dot of concealer (the same shade as your skin) on it or just around the edges to disguise the redness. This is the best way to conceal a pimple and is better than putting a large blob of concealer on top, which can often just draw attention to the area.

More than a pimple?? Acne can be caused by a number of things–hormones, digestive issues, stress and more. There are a number of things you can try though. I would recommend that, in addition to everything listed in this chapter, you also see a naturopath.

★ Your body has skin too

The skin on your body will also benefit from some love and care. It's a little tougher than the skin on your face, so you'll need to use products on your body that are a bit heavier and more nourishing.

Natural deodorant

I think deodorant is a **must switch** item. You just have to switch to natural. There have been links between regular deodorant and breast cancer, with our armpits being so close to our lady lumps, and we have a bunch of lymph nodes that hang out in our armpits too. One thing our body is supposed to do is sweat. So spraying a cloud of antiperspirant deodorant (antiperspirant means it stops the body from sweating) into your pits each day deliberately stops your body from doing something it's supposed to do.

As we learnt earlier from our naturopath Kasey, if you stop the body from sweating properly then it can look at other ways to expel toxins, which can lead to skin conditions. Check out my DIY deodorant recipe on Page 97 or start trying some natural brands today.

Still want to spray something when you're at school? Make-up an essential oil spritzer using a clean spray bottle, some filtered water and a few drops of your favourite essential oil blend (find our favourites at shinefromwithinhq.com). It will smell so much better than a bottle of chemical-laden body fragrance and will have the added benefit of uplifting your mood!

Body brushing

Body brushing is where you use a dedicated 'body brush' in circular motions all over your naked body. This helps to get the lymphatic system working. The lymphatic system runs alongside your blood vessels, but doesn't have a heart to pump it like the blood does. This is why it is good to help it along with a body brush. If you have any signs of cellulite this will be very beneficial, as it can help to move any fatty deposits out of the body.

Dry body brushing stimulates circulation, increases cell renewal, removes dead skin, improves texture and more. Google 'body brush' to see what a brush looks like or find one in your local supermarket, health food store or pharmacy.

Follow these steps:

1. Do it first thing in the morning before your shower.
2. Don't wet the skin or the brush—it's best to do it dry.
3. Always brush towards the heart in long, smooth strokes.
4. Start at your feet, then ankles, calves, thighs, stomach, buttocks, back, hands and arms.
5. Do lighter strokes around your chest and avoid the face and neck.
6. Then jump in the shower to remove any of the dead skin cells that you've stirred up.
7. As you are going along, be grateful to each part of your body and the amazing job that it does.

Daily massage

Wouldn't you **love** a massage every day? The great news is you can give yourself a full body massage every single day and it won't take up any more time than your usual 'shower and get ready for the day' routine.

Every day when you get out of the shower, give yourself a full-body massage:

1. While your skin is still damp from your morning shower, apply a body oil. (I like to make up my own with a sweet almond oil base and some essential oils that will act like a beautiful perfume at the same time.)
2. Just like the dry body brushing, start at your feet and work your way up towards your heart, vigorously massaging the oil into your body as you go. Be a little rough with yourself here, massaging your shoulders, arms and every single beautiful part of you.

The perfect golden tan

I'm sure you've heard it a million times before: protection from the sun is important. But in saying that, most experts agree that getting 10–15 minutes of sun every day is good for you. Vitamin D, which the beautiful sun provides, is good for our health and can also improve our mood. Unfortunately, sunscreens can be full of lots of chemicals, so it's best to stay out of the sun in the middle of the day (between 10am and 3pm) and choose a natural sunscreen to wear when you're out and about.

Hint: the natural sunscreen will feel thick and leave a white film, because it's sitting on top of the skin to protect it. The fancy, fragrant, misty ones that you don't notice are usually full of chemicals that can be harmful for your beautiful bod.

If you want a golden tan but don't want to end up all leathery and wrinkly when you're older, then find a fake tan that you like. Just make sure you apply it properly, so you don't have patches and orange hands!

When I was modelling, the perfect tan every day of the week was essential. Here's how to apply fake tan like a pro:

1. Before applying your tan, exfoliate, shave your legs and underarms, then pat your skin dry.
2. For a more even tan, moisturize **only** your elbows, knees, belly button and ankles, because they are the driest parts of the body and so will absorb more of the tan (going extra orange if you skip this step!).
3. If you are applying it to your face, also moisturise that area, as you don't want to it to be too thick on the face.
4. Make sure you cover your hands in moisturiser too, so you don't end up with orange palms.
5. Once the moisturiser has soaked into your hands, squeeze a decent amount of tan on your hands and rub together.

Start to apply all over the body, starting from the bottom up, avoiding the bottom of your feet.

6. Wash your hands, particularly in between your fingers. Make sure you're careful not to get water on another part of your body to avoid water marks on your tan.

7. Dry your hands with a towel and then, using the same towel, which will now be slightly damp, blend the tan from your wrist to your hand so that you don't end up with a line from when you have washed your hands.

8. It's also good to blend the colour from your ankles to your feet.

9. Moisturise your skin every day after you have tanned, so it lasts as long as possible.

Try this! ➤ Want shiny, pearly teeth?

Coffee, black tea, cigarettes, cola and red wine can all contribute to stained teeth. If you're not brushing regularly and looking after your mouth hygiene, then it doesn't matter what you eat—you could be slowly staining your teeth (not to mention bad breath, which is gross!).

So first things first. Ensure you are brushing and flossing at least twice a day. A soft toothbrush is best. And let the brush do the work; you don't need to get too aggressive!

Oil pulling

For some extra love, try oil pulling first thing in the morning. Oil pulling removes all the mucous, bacteria and toxins from your body through your saliva. It's also been known to make your teeth whiter and shinier, so give it a go!

Here's how: before you eat, drink or brush your teeth in the morning, put a tablespoon of oil into your mouth. (I like using coconut oil; in summer it's already liquefied, but in winter I just pop it into my mouth solid and it turns to liquid pretty quickly.) Swish it around, pulling it through your teeth as you go. This will feel totally weird at first and you'll find that your jaw and mouth get tired straightaway. Over time, you should be able to do it for up to twenty minutes! It's a great thing to do first thing in the morning, while stretching or going for a walk. Once you're done, spit it all out (don't swallow!) then rinse your mouth out or brush your teeth before eating or drinking.

Tip for extra white teeth

Try cleaning your teeth with a charcoal powder. Get a charcoal capsule and break it onto your toothbrush or find a dedicated charcoal scrub for teeth. You can usually get both from a health food store.

DIY SKINCARE RECIPES

~

Let's have some fun making delicious beauty products!

Citrus body and foot scrub

Ingredients:
4 tbsp raw sugar
2 tbsp poppy seeds
3 tbsp apricot kernel or sweet almond oil
6 drops each of lime, lemon and mandarin oil (or your own special blend!)

Method:
Mix the dry ingredients together and then add the oils. Store in an amber glass jar. Keep your beautiful body scrub out of sunlight, so that it lasts a few weeks.

Hint: Wrap your pretty jar up with ribbon or string and give it as a beautiful, handmade gift!

Fresh fruit face mask

Ingredients:
1 strawberry (organic and washed)
¼ banana
2 slices cucumber (a facial isn't complete without lying back with cucumbers over your eyes!)

Method:
Mash the ingredients together. Apply to a clean face, doing your best not to eat it (because it smells like a delicious smoothie on your face)! Leave it on for a few minutes (you may need to lie down so you can let it all soak in and work its magic). Then rinse (or lick!) it off.

Hint: Get your besties around and have a fruity spa day together!

Why are these ingredients so magical for your skin?

Strawberries: a natural source of salicylic acid. SA is a common anti-acne ingredient, used to clean out pores and get rid of blackheads without drying out the skin. They are also a great natural exfoliant. Yay strawberries!

Bananas: packed full of vitamins, bananas are also soothing and moisturising for the skin. They also add a lovely coolness to the mask and keep it all together.

Pink face lift mask

Ingredients:
1 tbsp pink clay
1 organic green teabag
1 tsp fresh grated apple
2 drops rosehip oil

Method:

Steep the green teabag in just enough water to cover it for one hour. Add a tablespoon of the green tea concentrate to a bowl, then add the rest of the ingredients. You want it to be like a paste that can be easily applied to your face—not too runny and not too dry. If it's a little runny, add more clay. If it's too dry, add more green tea concentrate.

Why are these ingredients so magical for your skin?

Pink clay: clays are wonderful for absorbing oil and extracting impurities from your skin. There are lots of different types and colours but pink clay is an ideal balance for those with sensitive skin who need a little bit of 'oil vacuuming' and gentle exfoliation. For something even more gentle, go for white kaolin clay. If you have oily skin and would like to use something more powerful, try bentonite clay or green clay.

Green tea: high in antioxidants which protect the skin, as well as enzymes, amino acids, phytochemicals, B vitamins, folate, potassium, magnesium and caffeine. Green tea has been shown to rejuvenate the skin, making it shiny and beautiful. If you put a couple of used green teabags in the fridge for 30 minutes then place them over your eyes, it can even help to reduce puffy eyes and dark circles! Green tea also has antibacterial properties, helping to fight acne-causing bacteria on the skin.

Apples: full of antioxidants and vitamins that help to lighten, brighten and soothe your skin. They have a high content of collagen and elastin, which keeps the skin looking plump and youthful. Apples are also very hydrating for the skin and have cooling properties, soothing your skin to provide relief from acne or sunburn.

Rosehip oil: protects skin cells from sun damage and is also a natural source of essential fatty acids (omega-3, 6 and 9), which help to repair and regenerate damaged skin tissue. Rosehip oil is also a natural source of vitamin C, which brightens the skin and restores skin tone.

Apple cider vinegar toner

Ingredients:
1 tbsp apple cider vinegar
4 tbsp water

Method:
Mix ingredients together and store in a glass container in the fridge. To apply, dip a cotton pad into the mixture and gently rub over your face, avoiding your eyes. Do not rinse after use.

To ensure that this will be okay on your skin, make sure you do a patch test first, to see how your skin responds. Do not apply the apple cider vinegar directly onto your skin—make sure it's diluted in water, as the recipe recommends.

Why are these ingredients so magical for your skin?

Apple cider vinegar: balances the natural pH of the skin, which is often disturbed after cleansing. It also helps to break up the bonds between dead skin cells, gently removing them so that your pores do not get blocked (often the cause of blackheads and pimples).

DIY deodorant

Ingredients:
¼ cup bicarbonate soda
8 drops essential oil blend

Method:

1. Fill a clean container about a quarter full with some of the bicarb soda. (A used spice shaker container works really well, or a small tub with a screw-top that easily fits into your bag.)
2. Add a couple of drops of the essential oil blend.
3. Add some more bicarb soda.
4. Add a few more drops of the essential oil blend.
5. Repeat until you've used your ingredients and/or have filled your container.
6. Close the lid and shake.

To use, sprinkle or scoop out about ½ tsp of the mixture, using two or three fingers. Wet two or three fingers on your other hand and blend together to form a clear paste. Apply to armpits straight after your shower.

Note: This will not stop you from sweating, but will neutralise odours so that you smell fresh. Do not use straight after shaving and discontinue use if you feel any irritation.

Cool green mask

Ingredients:
½ avocado
1 tsp chia seeds
1 tblsp oats

Method:
Mash the avocado and mix in the chia seeds and oats. Add a little water, if you feel it needs it. Smooth onto clean damp skin. Leave for 10-15 mins. Rinse thoroughly.

Why are these ingredients so magical for your skin?

Avocado: filled with numerous fats and oils that are great internally, avocado is also wonderful to use externally. It will help to soften and moisturise the skin.

Chia seeds: filled with omega-3, an essential fatty acid, as well as antioxidants.

Oats: are soothing and will also give your skin a light exfoliation.

FIND YOUR STYLE

Buy less, choose well, make it last.

Vivienne Westwood,
British fashion designer and businesswoman

Ever stressed out about what to wear? Ever spent what feels like **hours** trying to get ready, trying on everything in your closet and deciding you have absolutely nothing? I get it! Fashion changes so fast, and we want to stand out but also fit in. And even if you don't care about fashion **at all**, you still need to get dressed in the morning. So hopefully I can help you out with that.

It's all about the feels . . . the trick to feeling like you've nailed your outfit is all about feeling comfortable and confident wearing it. And once you've started working on shining on the inside (go back and read the first half of this book if you haven't already!), then you can use style as a vehicle to share all of your awesomeness with the world.

To me, that's what style is all about. That's what makes fashion fun. It's the way you can share with the world **how you're feeling that day.**

★ Style vs fashion

*Dressing well is kind of good manners, if you ask me.
When you're standing in a room, your effect is the
same as a chair's effect, or a sculpture's. You're part of
someone's view, you're part of that world, and so you
should dress well. I find it's a show of respect to try to
put on your best face and look as good as you can.*

Tom Ford, American fashion designer

So, what's the difference between fashion and style?

Fashion lumps us all together, is constantly changing and makes us feel like we're always playing catch-up. That's the point of it–to make us feel inadequate so we buy more stuff. Style, however, is an **attitude**. It's the way we express ourselves to the world.

There was a cool study conducted at Northwestern University back in 2012[12], which found that what we wear has a direct impact on **how** we do things. They tested this using lab coats! People who wore a lab coat and were told that it was a doctor's coat were more attentive in the experiments than people who didn't wear a lab coat or were told that the lab coat was just a painter's coat.

This explains why we can feel more confident and beautiful wearing an expensive brand name outfit. It's not necessarily the outfit itself, but the symbolic meaning we give to it. ('I'm cooler because I'm wearing this brand!') Make sense?

---

12 Galinsky, A. and Adam, H. *Enclothed Cognition.* Journal of Experimental Social Psychology, ISSN: 0022-1031, Vol: 48, Issue: 4, Page: 918-925 https://doi.org/10.1016/j.jesp.2012.02.008

★ Finding your style

Your style will change depending on your mood, the occasion you're dressing for and a bunch of other reasons I'll touch on in a moment. But you get to decide how it represents you. You get to make a choice every morning about how you want to look and, most importantly, how you want to **feel**.

Some mornings I wake up and realise that I'm feeling a little fragile. On those days, I don't put on my most colourful, loudest outfit, because I don't feel like making a statement or drawing attention. On those days I'll wear darker colours, relaxed silhouettes and just kind of float on through the day.

Other days, I want to share bright colours and happiness with everyone I meet! I want to smile and socialise. I feel more 'summery.' On those days, I'll wear my favourite dress or take a risk by putting an outfit together that I haven't tried before. I'll go wild!

You get to make the same choice. Regardless of how you feel on a particular day, you'll probably have some colours, styles or patterns that you just feel are 'you.' Whether you care

---

13 Pine, Karen. (2014). Mind What You Wear.

about fashion or not, you're already telling a story with your clothes and it's often how we find our 'tribe' at first glance. We see others dressed in a similar way to us and we feel like we belong with them.

All sorts of things about your life will influence your style and the story you tell. For example:

- your location
- your favourite activities
- who you hang out with
- your culture and background
- how you feel about your body
- your personality (extroverted vs introverted/ playful vs precise, which we touch on later in the book, starting on page 135)

★ Take shine-worthy action

Take a moment to answer these questions on the lines below:

1. What or who influences your style at the moment?
2. How would you describe your style?
3. What are your favourite items of clothing?
4. What are you trying to portray to the world through your style, even if you didn't realise it before?
5. What are your 'happy' clothes?

1. ....

2. ....

3. ....

4. ....

5. ....

★ *Get the look*

Let's work on how to put an outfit together . . . your parents will be happy about this one!

Putting together a great outfit starts with an organised wardrobe. Think of your wardrobe as a gateway to your most shiny self. Keep it clean and organised, so you feel good every time you look at it. Sort through your clothes. You want to organise your wardrobe so it's easy to find exactly what you need. For example, all of your jeans neatly folded on a particular shelf with all of your other bottoms.

Everyone puts their outfits together differently, but start with one item that you feel drawn to that day. It could be a necklace, top, pants, dress or shoes. Then build from there, being conscious of how the items will balance each other.

Here are some 'rules' to keep in mind:

- Create a **total look**. Hair, make-up, shoes and accessories are just as important as the clothes we wear and all work together to finish off a look.
- You don't need to be a slave to fashion—use what's 'in' as a guide and pick out pieces that suit your body shape and your own individual style.
- Wear what feels comfortable—you can always tell when someone isn't 100% comfortable in what they are wearing— they fidget and tug at their clothes, usually looking less confident.
- Build your wardrobe, starting with basics that won't go out of fashion. These are the pieces that are worth spending a bit of money on and can be worn with lots of different things. For example, jeans, basic tees, denim shorts, a blazer or cardigan.
- You don't have to spend a lot of money to dress well. Understanding fashion is a skill like any other. Take time to

'research' fashion trends or your favourite style muse and see how others dress by flicking through magazines and looking online. Street style blogs and social media feeds of your style icons are great for following what everyday people are wearing and how they pull it all together.

- Upgrade your existing wardrobe. Before throwing anything out, consider whether it can be altered e.g. cut sleeves off a top or cut off jeans to make cute shorts. I'm not very handy with a sewing machine so cutting things up is all I can manage without going to a tailor! If not, give it away, have a swap night or sell it. One girl's hand-me-downs are another girl's treasure!

- Wear appropriate underwear that cannot be seen under your outfit. G-strings and seamless underwear, like boylegs and T-shirt bras, are great staples.

- Get your bra fitted properly—if you don't wear the right size it can cause damage down the track and look funny under your clothes. Most lingerie stores and some underwear departments of big chain stores have trained staff who will happily help you out with this for free. Don't worry, they literally see hundreds of boobs a day!

- Always try before you buy.

- Get your clothes out the night before, so you're not stressed in the morning—help the future **you** out!

- Consider where the garment came from—who made it, how far it travelled, the impact it may have had on the environment, etc. Every time we buy something, we are essentially voting for the type of world we want to live in. Support businesses that are doing positive things. More on that in a moment . . .

- Dress to flatter your body shape—more on that coming up too.

★ Take shine-worthy action

Spend an afternoon in your wardrobe with your favourite tunes playing. The idea here is to figure out what you love, what you can alter and what you can donate. So you'll need to make three piles.

Pump up the volume and try **everything** on—your very own fashion show. Try different combinations too; see what can go with what. Just by doing this one step, you'll find a whole bunch of new outfits that you didn't even know existed in your wardrobe!

Be brutal. If you haven't worn something for the past year, really ask yourself if you'll wear it again. If not, add it to the donate pile. It's okay if your donate pile is bigger than the rest, because what you'll be left with is a wardrobe full of clothes you **love**. No more sorting through the stuff you hate to find the things you love. They will all just be there, right in front of you.

★ Kind fashion

Now I know you give a hoot about our beautiful Mama Earth, children in developing countries and animals—of course you do! So, let me **empower** you to make fashion choices that are kind.

How do clothes arrive in our wardrobe . . .

It was during a fashion show, modelling fur coats made of fox, mink and rabbit, that I had a lightbulb moment: 'Hang on, these were once cute, furry animals!' That moment changed me forever. I started to think about how the clothes we wear came to be.

Think about your favourite tee, pair of jeans or shoes. See if you can find out:

• Who made them?

- Where were they made?
- What material are they made of?
- Were they dyed with chemicals?
- Have they travelled halfway around the world to make it into your wardrobe?
- Were children younger than you forced to make them?
- Did animals suffer or die to create them?

I did some digging and found out that:

- There are 168 million child labourers aged from 5-17 years.[14]
- More than a billion rabbits are skinned to create fur coats each year.[15]
- Leather for shoes, bags, etc. takes a huge process to create and in 2016 over 300 million hides and skins were produced from sheep and lambs, bovines (cows and buffalos) and goats and kids.[16] In Australia, over one million kangaroos are killed each year for meat and, strangely, to make soccer shoes![17] It starts with breeding and raising the animals, transporting feed, removing animal waste, powering housing and killing facilities, the use of vaccines and antibiotics, removing carcasses and transferring pelts (skins). At the tannery, the skins are sorted, soaked, fleshed, tanned, wrung, dried, cleaned,

---

14 *Global Estimates and Trends of Child Labour.* International Labour Organization, 2012 http://www.ilo.org/wcmsp5/groups/public/@ed_norm/@ipec/documents/publication/wcms_221881.pdf

15 United Nations, Food and Agriculture Organization, *The Rabbit: Husbandry, Health and Production* (Rome: United Nations, 1997). http://www.fao.org/docrep/t1690e/t1690e00.htm

16 United Nations Food and Agriculture Organization, *World statistical compendium for raw hides and skins, leather and leather footwear 1999-2015*, FAOSTAT Database http://www.fao.org/3/a-i5599e.pdf

17 Population, quota and harvest statistics for NSW, QLD, SA and WA commercial harvest areas http://www.environment.gov.au/system/files/pages/d3f58a89-4fdf-43ca-8763-bbfd6048c303/files/kangaroo-statistics-states-2018.pdf

trimmed, buffed, dried again, finished (with loads of chemicals so they don't disintegrate while you're walking in them) and then transported to the garment maker, wholesaler and so on.[18] Some people think leather is just a by-product of the meat industry, but this isn't always the case. Many animals are raised specifically for leather.

- We throw away a **lot** of clothes each year, all around the world. In the US, they throw away 13 million tons of textiles (fabrics/clothing) each year[19]; Australians send 85% of their clothing to landfill each year[20]; and in the UK, they are throwing away £25 million a year by sending clothes to landfill.[21] Yikes!

- Experts suggest we're living in a 'fast fashion' world, where we just want more, more, more, cheap, cheap, cheap. We need to be working towards slow and sustainable fashion instead. Makes sense, right?

Unfortunately or thankfully, depending on how you look at it, we can't just hang out naked. So clothing will always be a part of our lives. But we can take this knowledge and be mindful about what we add to our wardrobe. We can think twice before we buy a $4 tee just because it's on sale (when you and I both know we'll only wear it once and then it will fall apart)!

To be a **modern, kind human being** in a fast fashion world:

✓ Ask questions and be curious.
✓ Watch documentaries like *The True Cost* to learn more.

---

18 PETA, *Environmental Hazards of Leather* https://www.peta.org/issues/ animals-used-for-clothing/leather-industry/leather-environmental-hazards/
19 https://www.onegreenplanet.org/ news/13-million-tons-of-clothes-are-filling-up-our-landfills/
20 https://textilebeat.com/aussies-send-85-of-textiles-to-landfill/
21 https://www.businessgreen.com/bg/news/2204863/ uk-throwing-out-gbp25m-a-year-by-sending-clothes-to-landfill

✓ Hang up your clothes as soon as you take them off. They'll be less stinky and less creased, so you won't need to wash and iron them as often.

✓ Don't wash your jeans too often. Yep, you can use me as an excuse for **not** washing your jeans. Instead, spot clean any stains with an old toothbrush, like Levi's CEO Chip Bergh does.

✓ Get some natural laundry detergent. A big impact a piece of clothing has on the environment is often in the wearing phase—washing, drying and ironing.

✓ Line dry your clothes where possible, instead of putting them in the dryer.

✓ Look out for certifications on the label (like 'certified organic') to suggest an item is using organic fabrics; or 'fair trade' which means they've paid their workers a fair wage.

✓ Check out op shops for one-of-a-kind bargains.

✓ Don't throw your old clothes in the bin. Take them to an op shop. Recycle them. You can even take them into big clothing stores like fashion giant H&M, where they'll recycle them for you while giving you a discount on your next purchase.

★ Take shine-worthy action

Next time you go shopping, ask yourself these questions:

• Do I really need this? (Keep a list on your phone of things you need to add to your wardrobe.)
• Do I have something to wear it with?
• Will it last?
• Do I freakin' **love** it?

And then see what you can find out about the item of clothing. Check the inside label to see what it's made of. Cotton?

Polyester? Is it organic? Does it say 'fair trade'? Ask the shop assistant if you're having trouble. She may look at you blankly; but even if you don't get the answers you're looking for, you will have alerted her to the fact that you care about this stuff and she should too.

★ Body shapes + silhouettes

We all look different and have differently-shaped bodies, thank goodness! It would be a boring world if we all looked the same. Our choice of clothing can be a beautiful way to highlight our own natural shape. And this section of the book is about **celebrating** your shape, your quirks, your individuality.

So first, what shapes or silhouettes are you drawn to? Do you always buy a particular style of dress? What shapes do you feel comfortable and confident in? Chances are, these are styles that naturally suit your particular body shape. Use the info below as a guide, but don't let it restrict you—wear whatever you like, baby.

When it comes to choosing styles that suit your particular beautiful body shape, it all comes down to balance. Our eyes love to see things in balance—not just in fashion, but also in architecture, make-up, food styling, flower arrangements, etc. We're just drawn to it!

Which shape are you? Read each of the below descriptions as there are lots of hints and tips in each one that could apply to you!

Apple shape

Apples tend to have:

- a broader/wider back and upper body
- medium to large bust (boobs)

- not much of a defined waist
- slimmer hips, thighs, legs and ankles

Styling tips for an apple:

- Vertical lines are your best friends!
- Use soft draping and ruching that skims, rather than clings, to the tummy.
- Go for clean, tailored lines to streamline your body and show off your slim legs.
- Wear deep necklines to minimise your bust (V-necks, scoop necks and sweetheart necklines).
- Wear garments with shape through the sides and back (darts, seams etc.) but without waist definition.
- Wear tunic style garments, as they skim over the tummy and show off slender legs.
- Wear fitted pants and skirts, to show off slender hips and thighs.
- Use necklaces and scarves or open necklines (cardigans and jackets) to create a vertical shape down your body. (This balances out your beautiful bust.)
- Avoid wearing billowing or wide sleeves, as this can broaden your bust and shoulders.
- Avoid wearing oversized and super loose-fitting clothes, which will make you look bigger than you are.

Column shape

Columns tend to have:

- shoulders, waist and hips approximately the same width
- not much of a defined waist
- average to small bust
- long, lean limbs

Styling tips for a column:

- Show off your lean limbs.
- Focus on styles that can be wrapped and tied to create a waistline.
- Wear styles that have wider shoulders, to make the waist appear narrower.
- Wear skirts that have a lean pencil shape or A-line.
- Wear belted and fitted styles, to give the illusion of a defined waist.
- Wear sleeveless styles, to show off your lean arms.
- Wear straight leg pants and slim-fitting skirts, to show off your lean hips and thighs.
- Don't be scared to wear shapely, waisted clothes, to give yourself more of an hourglass shape.
- Avoid wearing anything cropped—it can make you look short in the torso.

Hourglass shape

Hourglasses tend to have:

- shoulders and hips about the same width apart
- medium to large bust
- smaller waist
- curvy hips and bum, but slender thighs

Styling tips for an hourglass:

- Look for styles that fit to your gorgeous curves—avoid anything that is roomy in the waist.
- If you have a fuller bust or are a larger size, keep the look streamlined, with tailored panels or simple silhouettes.
- Lean pencil or A-line skirts are flattering—think 50s!

- Deep necklines minimise a larger bust (V-necks, scoop necks and sweetheart necklines).
- Define your waist with fitted garments or a belt.
- Chunky jewellery and shoes will balance out your gorgeous curves.
- Avoid hiding your curves with shapeless blouses, jumpers and jackets.
- Avoid high necklines which will increase the surface area of your bust, making it look larger.
- Avoid wearing tops and dresses that hang off your bust— they will hide your small waist and make you look bigger than you are.

Pear Shape

Pears tend to have:

- small to average bust
- neat waist
- shoulders narrower than hips and thighs
- weight in their bottom half

Styling tips for a pear:

- Avoid tops or tunics that finish at your widest part.
- Balance out your hips with a wider neckline or shoulder line (boatneck, sweetheart neckline, fluted or cap sleeves).
- Wear A-line skirts and dresses with a flare that skims out over hips and thighs.
- Define your upper body and waist with fitted tops and belts.
- Skim over your hips and thighs in wide-leg pants.
- Chunky jewellery and shoes will balance out your gorgeous curves.

- Avoid shoes with ankle straps. They cut off your legs and make you look shorter than you are.

To download pictures and information sheets of each body shape, head to shinefromwithinhq.com.

Now break these rules and wear whatever you want!

BEAUTIFUL HAIR

★ Don't set your hair on fire!

Ever seen those flammable warning signs on hairspray? Scary! Just as we covered in skin care and nutrition, you want to avoid as many chemicals as possible on the hair, because hair follicles are like the pores in your skin. My friends at EverEscents Organic Hair Care suggest we watch out for the following chemicals and avoid them when possible:

- silicone (dimethicone, cyclopentasiloxane)
- paraben (propylparaben, methylparaben)
- formaldehyde (DMDM hydantoin, diazolidinyl urea)
- plastic (PVP polymer, VA copolymer)
- artificial fragrances (perfume, parfum)
- animal-tested ingredients (search for 'cruelty-free' labels)

Ingredients to look for in beautiful hair care products:

- ✓ essential oils
- ✓ herbal extracts
- ✓ certified organic ingredients
- ✓ plant-based ingredients

★ What's your hair type?

Just like the rest of your beautiful body and skin, your hair will be unique to you. And while it seems like **everyone** with straight hair wants curly hair and vice versa, the more we can work with our own hair, rather than force it to do something else, the healthier our locks will be! Your hair might be:

- oily/dry/sensitive
- coloured/natural
- thin/thick
- long/short
- curly/straight

Based on these different elements, your hair will need to be treated and cared for differently. For example, if your hair is quite oily and gets shiny very quickly, then you may need to wash it every day. If it's dry, then you could go a few days without washing it and may need a more moisture-intense shampoo and conditioner. Everyone is different.

However, there some general guidelines we should all follow:

- Use natural products whenever possible.
- Comb or brush your hair while **dry** to remove all the knots, before jumping in the shower.
- Brushing your hair while wet causes breakage and damage; use a wide-tooth comb instead.
- Get a haircut regularly. It will grow faster when the damaged ends have been snipped off.
- Don't tie your hair up while wet. Hair is delicate while still wet and expands as it's drying.
- Don't tie your hair up too tightly, as this might cause breakage. Try tying your hair up in different styles, so you're not adding stress to the same section of hair every day.

- Try not to use heating tools on your hair every day. (I know you might love your straightener, but give your hair a break sometimes!) Before using heat tools, ensure your hair is absolutely dry (there shouldn't be steam coming from your hair). And once you've styled it the way you want, leave it alone. The moisture in your fingers will ruin the look super fast if you keep touching it!

Feel like your hair is damaged?

Get yourself a natural treatment or apply your own, using coconut oil. Wash your hair, towel dry and then apply coconut oil and cover with a shower cap for about half an hour, to let it soak in. Then jump back in the shower to rinse out. Your hair will feel so luscious!

Are you a swimmer?

Prior to swimming, protect your hair by applying a few drops of Moroccan Argan Oil from roots to ends.

* Colour me happy

Hair colour can be so much fun! But most of it is not natural, so keep these tips in mind:

- Avoid cheap hair colour and look out for more natural brands at your health food store or hairdresser.
- Reduce the number of times you colour your hair.
- Go for colours that are similar to your natural colour—it's when you drastically change your colour that you can do lots of damage. (Burning scalp, anyone?)

- If you want something fun like a pop of pink in your hair, go for temporary 'spray on/paint on' products that wash out after a few washes (some are even formulated with vegetable dyes—bonus!) or hair 'chalk' that will wash straight out in your next shower.

MAKE-UP SECRETS

★ Natural make-up 101

By now I think you know it's gotta be natural. But let's face it, make-up that's natural but doesn't look any good is going to get discarded pretty quickly, right? So I always love using professional make-up artist ranges that don't compromise on quality. They might be more expensive upfront, but they'll last wayyyyy longer, because you won't need to use as much.

Light matters

Make sure you have a well-lit area to apply your make-up. Natural light makes a huge difference. Under yellow or fluorescent lights, your make-up will probably look awesome in the mirror, but then not so great when you step outside or vice versa. If you don't have great lighting where you do your make-up, just make sure you head to a window or outside to check it. A final check in the car before you step out works well.

Look after your brushes

Your make-up brushes are the perfect breeding ground for bacteria. So, unless you want congestion and pimples, keeping your brushes clean is super-duper important. Gently wash your brushes with a mild shampoo once a week, wring them out gently and place them with bristles up in a cup to dry for the day (preferably in the sun, but the bathroom windowsill is fine too).

Don't share mascara

You shouldn't share any of your make-up, brushes or lipsticks with your friends. (Sharing is caring, but not sharing diseases and oily skin—eww!) And you **definitely** shouldn't share your mascara. Our eyes are super sensitive. If you've ever seen kids with conjunctivitis, you'll be quick to say, 'I love you but get your own mascara!' to your besties.

Try this! ➤ **Matching colour** might seem obvious, but I bet you've seen someone with foundation that doesn't match—they look too orange, too white or just not quite right. Making sure you have the right shade of foundation is super important.

To match your foundation, test it on your **face**. Not your wrist, hand, arm, neck or any other body part. Apply quite a bit of foundation to your cheek—if it's the right colour you won't really see it, but if it's the wrong colour you should be able to tell straightaway.

Lipstick and eye shadow colours to suit different skin tones:

- For cool, neutral and olive tones, rosy pinks, berry hues and blue-toned reds work well.
- For beige, warm and olive tones, peachy pinks, corals and warm reds work best (but have a play around and see what you love).

But wait . . . what's my skin tone? So glad you asked!

Take off your make-up and look at your face side-on in the mirror. You'll see pinkish/blue tones if you have cool undertones. And you'll see yellow/gold tones if you have warmer undertones.

★ What brand?

There is no shortage of make-up brands and they all spend a fortune to try and convince you that you **need** what they're selling. You don't. You're perfect just the way you are.

The whole point of make-up is to enhance your natural features—not to mask your beautiful face. On YouTube tutorials, you often see someone really caking it on thickly. That's fine if you're sitting in your PJs at home, with a perfectly-lit beauty light set up on your computer. But I can guarantee you that the gorgeous girls in those vids probably wouldn't actually leave the house wearing that much make-up. So learn as much as you can from YouTube but also play around in the mirror at home.

Go for natural brands. Then your skin will actually feel better after wearing make-up, rather than feeling gross at the end of the day. I've tried every brand you can throw at me and I can tell you that the big brands just have awesome marketing campaigns. Look for mineral make-up and go for a professional range, because then a little goes a LOONNGG way so it will last much longer. For our fave natural brands that look amazing too, head to the shinefromwithinhq.com

IRL ➤ Not sure if make-up is for you? We're all different, so do what feels right. I've had beautiful students who are dead against make-up and the idea that women are 'supposed' to wear it. I respect and admire this view. I've also had students who are creative and artistic and their face is their canvas. Decide for yourself.

I can go weeks without wearing make-up and then other times I just love playing with it and will wear it every day. Think of it as a fun way to express yourself. It usually protects your skin from the sun too (make sure it has SPF 15+ on the packaging).

Make-up can make you feel more confident. Not because you feel like you need to wear it to be beautiful (that's the opposite of feeling confident), but because you did it yourself, are expressing yourself in an authentic way, and feel 'ready' for the day.

★ My parents won't let me wear make-up

I know lots of parents tell us we don't need make-up and (cue eye roll emoji) that's very sweet, but it can feel like they just don't get it sometimes. If everyone at school is wearing make-up and you don't, then you might feel like you stand out like a sore thumb. (Where did that saying come from anyway?)

If you really want to start experimenting with make-up but your parents are uncomfortable with it, that can feel really frustrating. But kicking up a stink about it probably won't help. Try having an open conversation about it with them instead.

Find out why they're uncomfortable. They may be worried about chemicals on your skin. They may feel like you're growing up too fast and think you look too old with make-up. They may have seen some girls down the road with the thickest black eyeliner ever and assume that that's the look you're going for. You can't help them feel more comfortable about it if you don't know what they're thinking. So calmly ask them, 'Why don't you want me to wear makeup?'

No matter what they say, respond with: 'Okay thanks, that helps me to understand where you're coming from.' Then walk away. This is key, because in the moment you might just want to argue with them. Instead, go back to your room and think about what they actually said. Then you can formulate your response with a clear head (rather than just snapping back at them).

Depending on their response, you could calm their nerves about it. For example:

- If they are worried about chemicals, then do your research and find an affordable, natural brand you can show them. There are heaps out there and I would highly recommend that you use natural brands anyway.
- If they are worried about how you'll apply it, perhaps you could ask to attend a one-day make-up course in your area, so that you can learn how to apply it (or read on to our next section on the step-by-step process). You could even sit down and watch some YouTube videos with your parents, to show them the look you're after.
- If they are worried about you leaving the house with a full face of make-up, let them know that you just want to practise and play around with make-up. You won't leave the house with it on until they feel comfortable. Note: Don't say that and then hide your make-up in your schoolbag to apply later in the day. If you want more independence and freedom, you have to demonstrate that you're an honest, responsible person.

Start **very minimal** with your make-up journey. A light dusting of foundation or a tinted moisturiser (both with high SPF to protect your skin from the sun) is a great place to start. Add a lip gloss and you're ready to go. You can build up from there for special occasions or a night out.

★ Step-by-step to the perfect day look

This is a great process to use for any make-up look you're going for. Just adjust the colours and how heavily you apply it for different occasions. The products described here are versatile ones that can be used in a number of ways.

You can create the entire look with a foundation, concealer, blush, three eye shadows (will also be used as eyeliner and eyebrow powder), mascara and lipstick or gloss:

1. **Start with the perfect base.** Make sure you've cleansed, toned and moisturised your skin first. If your skin is oily or dry/flaky to start with, it will be harder to create the perfect base.
2. **Apply primer** if you have it, otherwise your moisturiser can act as a primer.
3. **Apply a cream concealer**, using your ring finger or a concealer brush. Your ring finger usually works really well, as the warmth from your finger helps to blend the concealer in well. Apply it to any dark circles under your eyes, redness around your nose or any other little spots you want to cover. Just a **light** covering is best, as you're still going to apply foundation. If you don't have a concealer, just mix a little of your powder foundation with primer or moisturiser to make a thicker cream that you can use instead.
4. **Apply foundation.** A loose powder foundation is best, because you can mix it with primer to make a liquid or use

it dry. I love a range that gives me options! Using a kabuki brush, dip it into the powder, tap away any excess back into the container, then start to blend onto your face. Press the brush and use circular, buffing motions to blend it all in. Our make-up artist, Kylie Eustace, suggests that two fine coats are better than one thick coat. Make sure you blend your foundation out over your ears, down onto your neck (not much—you shouldn't need to if your foundation is the right colour) and up into your hairline.

5. **Blush.** Using a mineral powder blush in a playful pink colour (and remembering to dust off the excess before applying as you did with the foundation), smile at yourself in the mirror. Those lovely round apples that appear on your cheeks when you smile are where you apply the blush. Blend it on in a circular, outward and upward motion.

6. **Eye shadow, Part 1.** Apply eye shadow in three steps, to highlight the brow bone and open up your eyes so they look even bigger and brighter. First select a soft, almost translucent colour to apply over your whole eyelid, all the way up to your eyebrows and on the inside corner of the eye. I love the colour Dream from Kylie's Mineral Goddess range on the *Shine From Within* website but any eye shadow palette with 3 or 4 colours will usually have a light, medium and dark colour. Choose the lightest one for this part. Imagine you have an invisible line going from the outside corner of your eye to the tail end of your eyebrow. Your shadow should stay within this line.

7. **Eye shadow, Part 2.** Next step is to emphasise the crease in your eye using a medium-tone eye shadow (I love the colour Bark for this). Using short strokes, press the eye shadow into the crease of your eye, starting at the outer corner and creating a 'C' shape, with the top part of the C going halfway along your crease or underside of your brow

bone and the bottom part of the C going along the top lash line. If you have larger eyes, you could extend your C all the way along the crease.

8. **Eye shadow, Part 3.** In just the outer corners of the eyes, emphasise the C shape with a matt dark brown or charcoal colour (I love Coffee Bean, but the darkest shade in your eye shadow palette will usually be perfect for this). Create a smaller C shape on the inside of the bigger C. This adds depth and contouring.

9. **Blend blend blend!** Using a small soft brush, blend your eye shadow doing small, circular strokes until your happy with it. If you feel like it's uneven or too dark, just keep blending and brushing over it. Tip: You can always add more but it's harder to take away, so **start light** and keep adding if you need to.

10. **Eyeliner.** Using a thin angle brush, moisten it in water and then dip it into your dark eye shadow pot, so that you create a cream or liquid liner. Draw a line on your hand to test how dark and thick the line will be. Angle your brush at 45° and press the brush along the top of your upper eye-lashes. Continue doing this until you have created a line right across the top of your upper lashes. Using the same brush, and without adding any more shadow to it, repeat the process underneath your lower eyelashes (but only about halfway along).

11. **Mascara.** Tilting your head back as you look at yourself in the mirror so that your eyes are partly closed, jiggle and sweep your mascara wand in an upward motion along the top lashes and then, without dipping your mascara wand back into the bottle, jiggle through the bottom lashes too. Note: Mascara on the lower eyelashes can cause a bit of a shadow, especially if you have quite long lashes, so you might like to skip this step.

12. **Eyebrows.** Using the same angle brush you used to apply your eyeliner, but with just dry shadow on it this time (a light-brown colour suits most colourings—we use the Bark colour on everyone from blonde to ginger to darker hair colours), create light, feathery short strokes along the eyebrows. I like to start by drawing a very light line across the top of the eyebrows and out to the corners, then do the little feathery strokes. The idea here is to fill in the eyebrows as though you are drawing on little hairs so they look really natural, rather than doing a strong outline and colouring it in.

13. **Lips.** Just as we discussed with fashion, it's all about balance in your make-up too. So if you've got very dark, smoky eyes, then a neutral lip will usually work well. If you're going for a really bright, bold lip, then keep the eye shadow soft and minimal. Or you can ignore that and go crazy with bright green eye shadow and bright purple lips if you want to! To apply your lipstick, put a bit of lipstick on a thin brush to outline the lips first and then fill in. Or go for a neutral gloss for a fresh look.

And there you have it! This takes us 2–3 hours to do together in a make-up class, but should take you about 10 minutes at home once you've got the hang of it. For a video lesson, head to www.shinefromwithinhq.com.

Try this! ➔ Go even more natural with food as make-up! Slice a beetroot in half and dab a sponge onto the freshly-cut part of the beetroot. Gently dab this onto your cheek for the perfect, natural blush.

You can also use a range of powders in your pantry as eye make-up: cacao or cocoa as your medium-brown eye shadow; spirulina if you want a green look on your eyes; charcoal powder mixed with a bit of coconut oil as your eyeliner; and frozen berries, slightly melted, as your lip gloss.

Have fun playing around!

MANI-PEDIS

★ The perfect manicure

Our beautiful hands do so much for us. Can you imagine getting through the day without them?

They are also on show every day and can often be one of the first parts of the body to show signs of ageing. Show some gratitude to them by taking time each day to massage your hands with a rich and nourishing hand cream (or just a bit of oil) and give yourself a full manicure every one or two weeks. If you don't have time for a full manicure, give yourself a weekly reshape and polish.

What you'll need:

- a bowl with warm water (add a couple of drops of essential oil if you wish)
- a handtowel
- an emery board (nail file)
- an orange stick (a stick with one pointy end and one slanting end—to push cuticles back)
- a tissue
- cotton balls

- nail polish remover
- a nail buffer (a block with four sides of successively finer grit)
- nail clippers
- nail polish (a base coat + colour or just a nude colour). Go for 'five-free' or 'seven-free' polishes, which contain fewer chemicals.

Getting prepared:

1. Take off any rings or bracelets.
2. Remove any old nail polish with cotton ball and nail polish remover.
3. Set up your station so that you don't need to move once you start, including your bowl with warm water.

Method:

1. Trim your nails using nail scissors or clippers, so that all of your nails are the same length.
2. File your nails using your emery board. Don't go back and forth across the top of the nail as this can weaken your nails. Instead, file your nails from one corner to the middle, then the opposite corner to the middle. Try to keep each nail the same shape, either square or rounded.
3. Soak your hands in your bowl of warm water for at least five minutes, until your fingers start to go wrinkly and your cuticles are soft. (Optional extra: Give yourself a hand scrub too, using the body scrub recipe from earlier in the book. Massage the scrub into your hands and forearms, then rinse off with warm water.)
4. Dry your hands on your handtowel.
5. Gentle push your cuticles back with the orange stick (never do this without soaking first). Your cuticles (the skin around the base of the nails) will usually bounce back but over time

the little half moon will show on all your nails, making your nails a little longer and encouraging healthy growth.

6. Clean underneath your nails using the pointy end of your orange stick and wipe any dirt on your tissue.

7. Buff your nails. Buffing strengthens your nails, removes ridges and ensures a smooth, shiny surface. Start with the roughest surface of the buffer, buffing in a back-and-forth motion as fast as you can on top of the nails. Then move to a smoother surface and repeat the motion.

8. At this point you may need to go back over each nail with a nail file, if you've noticed any sharp edges or roughage caught under the nail from when you filed earlier.

9. Moisturise your hands with a natural hand and cuticle cream. Take a few minutes to really massage the cream into your hands and into each cuticle. If you have any extra cream, massage it into your elbows, as they are one of the driest parts of the body.

10. Put a small amount of nail polish remover on a cotton ball and dab on top of each nail. This will ensure that no moisturiser is left on any of the nails, which can cause streaking when you start to paint.

11. Paint your nails. Start by painting your thumb first, then move your thumb out of the way (under the lip of the table) and paint your pinkie through to your index finger. This will prevent you from smudging the polish as you work your way along. Repeat on the other hand. Try to paint each nail in 3–4 steady strokes, starting with one in the middle, then one on each side. Start painting each stroke at the base of the nail but do not paint the cuticle—give it some breathing room. If you smudge any of your nails, just leave them and finish the rest.

12. If you have smudged any of your nails, hold a cotton ball between your second and third fingers (near the knuckles)

and apply a small amount of nail polish remover. Gently remove the polish from the nail that needs fixing and paint again. Or if you just need to fix a tiny bit, dip a cotton tip into the nail polish remover and dab it just where it needs fixing.

Manicure tips

- When painting your nails with a colour, start with a base coat to ensure they don't get stained (nails can go a funky yellow colour if you keep applying colour straight onto them).
- Make sure your nails are dry before applying a second coat of polish.
- Artificial nails, such as acrylic nails, will damage and weaken your nails. If you decide to get them, be prepared to invest money in having them redone regularly. And be careful— those places smell like a crazy chemical lair! So best to avoid them if you can.

Try this! ➤ Do you bite your nails? Time to stop! With so many germs under your nails, biting them is like licking a toilet seat—seriously! It's a habit like any other and habits can be broken. **You** can do anything!

Taking care of your nails, giving yourself regular manicures and filing your nails regularly (instead of biting) all help. Patience is also necessary as your nails grow at the rate of about 2.5mm per month, so when you are just starting to grow your nails it does take time.

Keep looking after them though and take note of when you go to bite them. If you are biting your nails while studying, then make sure you have a bottle of water and a bowl of seeds and nuts to snack on instead, so that you are doing something with your mouth and hands. If you are biting your nails when you are nervous, keep a nail file with you so that you can file your nails instead.

★ The perfect pedicure

To give yourself a pedicure, follow the same steps as above but with your feet! You won't need to do a pedicure as often as a manicure but it is a beautiful act of self-love and very relaxing.

You will need to soak your feet for a bit longer than your hands. Follow that step by using a pumice stone to remove any dead skin from your heels. You can also use the body scrub (see recipe on Page 93) to give yourself a foot scrub. Enjoy!

Tip: Give someone you love a pedicure—it's a wonderful experience to share with someone else.

After all this pampering and self-care, it's lovely to meet the new you! Hello there shiny woman!

Part 3
Shine in the world

HOW TO MAKE DECISIONS

When you're clear on your values you can make decisions that you feel really good about much more easily. So when a decision comes up, consider the following:

- What's most important to you?
- Which values should guide your decision in this particular situation?
- If you're not sure, what other information do you need to make your decision? Do you need to do some research (aka Google)?
- Do you need to consult with others to get their view?
- If so, how can you make sure you're getting a balanced viewpoint? (Maybe ask your parents as well as your friends, so you get a few different perspectives.)
- Do you need to write out a pros and cons list?

All of these questions will help you make a more informed decision. But above all, remember that **you** are the authority on you. Spiritual gurus and personal development junkies have been shouting this from the rooftops for decades. But this very important piece of information is usually kept from you—the teens, young ones, the selfie-generation, the kids who don't know anything just yet and should just be quiet and **listen**.

I know better. I know that you know better. You have opinions, values, experiences and a head on your shoulders. 'A brain in that noggin of yours,' as my dad would say. Sure, it's still growing but I'll tell you a secret: adults don't have it all figured out either.

★ Don't give away your power

Have you ever heard the word 'outsourcing'? Outsourcing is when businesses get other businesses to do the work for them. So a fashion label will outsource the manufacturing to another company, for example. Or a producer might outsource the editing of a movie to another company. It makes life easier. You outsource and someone else does it for you.

So while you should absolutely consult with others when making a decision, don't outsource it entirely. Some people **love** to outsource their decisions. If you outsource your decisions then you don't have to think. You just go along with whatever someone else suggests and then, bonus, you get to blame them when things don't go your way!

If you make decisions that way you **give your greatest power away**. Just give it away like it's nothing. One of the most amazing things about being human is that we can use our beautiful brains to analyse and make decisions. We can rise above the basic level of survival, of feeling hungry and going to gather food, like most animals, to go . . . actually, I don't feel good about this. I think **this** is what's most important. **This is who I want to be.**

So don't get caught out going with the easy (read 'lazy') option. The option where you just go along with your friends, even when you **know** it doesn't feel right to you. The option where you go to university and study what your parents told you to study, because it is easier than speaking up about what you truly want to do. If you do this, your life will pass you by and you'll get to eighty wondering what it was all for.

Bronnie Ware, author of *The Top Five Regrets of the Dying*, discovered that the top five regrets of people on their deathbed are:

1. I wish I'd had the **courage** to live a life true to myself, not the life others expected of me.
2. I wish I hadn't worked so hard.
3. I wish I'd had the courage to **express my feelings**.
4. I wish I'd stayed in touch with my friends.
5. I wish I had **let myself** be happier.

So heed these beautiful oldies' words. Find the courage now to live a life that's true to yourself.

By the way, that doesn't mean you shouldn't ask for help or advice. When making decisions in your life you have a duty to gather all the information, just like you're taught over and over again with those seemingly pointless assignments at school. Ask for advice. Chat with your friends about what they think. Listen to your parents. But then decide for yourself.

Yes, you're young. Yes, there will be other people around you who have more experience at life than you. But none of them have the experience of being **you** in this world. Only you know you. So getting clear on your own set of guidelines, the values that you hold dear, will help you to live up to the person you want to be. One that's kind, honest, beautiful inside and out, successful (in whatever way that happens to look for **you**), happy, free, etc.

Remember that the people in your life also get to do this for themselves too, even if you don't agree with them. We all have our own path; we have different values and that's totally okay.

FORGET FOMO AND LIVE YOUR WAY

You're at home, happy snuggled up on the couch watching your favourite movie. You've just had a bath, are sipping on some herbal tea and have a tub of your favourite coconut ice cream in hand. Life is perfect. It's just what you needed after a huge week.

Two minutes later and you're feeling anxious and upset, with a huge case of FOMO (fear of missing out). All because you decided to check your phone and saw some of your friends having a good time without you.

The struggle is real, right? FOMO can ruin a perfect day. On the other hand, JOMO (the **joy** of missing out) instantly turns the day into a positive experience.

So how do you go from FOMO to JOMO?

- **Make choices for you** and then stick by them. You were perfectly happy a moment ago!
- **Put boundaries in place** for yourself: don't check your phone so often; switch it to flight mode and enjoy the moment.
- **Accept that you can't do it all.** You can do anything you want, but not everything.

- **Check in with yourself** before committing to anything. How do you feel right now? What does your body need right now? Does it need a break from study and a walk on the beach? Does it need some laughs with your besties? Do you need to just buckle down and finish your assignment, so you can enjoy your weekend? Check in with yourself first.

- **Learn to say 'no'.** The best way to do this is to respond to any invitation: 'This sounds awesome but I'm just going to double-check I can do it.' That way you don't have to think on the spot, you're not being rude and you get to make a decision that's best for you.

- **Focus where your feet are.** It's easy to get swept up by FOMO when you're not truly present in where you are now. Just like we discussed earlier in the book, practice **presence**. Look around you right at this moment and find five things you can see, four things you can touch, three things you can hear, two things you can smell, and one thing you can taste.

Hint: This is a little tip for anxiety and helps to calm your body and mind, so that you can start to take some nice deep breaths.

- Remember that if you are experiencing FOMO because of something that's either happened in the past or is happening somewhere else right now, **you are actually missing out** on what's going on right in front of you.

There will be enough room for you.

Kathleen Buckley, yoga and meditation teacher,
sharing what she would tell her teen self

IRL ➤ Have a friend who suffers from anxiety? FOMO and so many other experiences can make a person feel anxious or upset. If they have a panic attack, you can support them by:

- being patient and calm (don't get annoyed when it takes them a moment to get through it)
- reminding them that you're there with them and they are not crazy
- having a chat with them about anything—if they can talk, then they can breathe
- encouraging them to exhale slowly through their nose, if they are struggling to breathe
- asking them if you can do anything to help them feel safe

Feeling anxious yourself? Try these tips:

- Focus on how you're feeling and let those feelings flow. Keep breathing and allow yourself to feel what you're feeling, rather than trying to get rid of the feelings or judging yourself for feeling that way. Acknowledging them often helps those feelings to ease.
- If you can, get on the floor into 'child's pose.' This is a yoga pose where you sit on your knees, placing your forehead on the floor in front of you and your arms down by your sides.
- Try seeing the world as though you are an owl. Owls have such big eyes that they are stuck in their sockets and can't move, which means they have excellent peripheral vision (can see things all around without moving their eyes). We have peripheral vision too, but spend most of our time focusing straight ahead. Using your peripheral vision and focusing on what is around you instantly brings you into

the present moment and brings a feeling of calm. Try it—pick a spot straight ahead and a little above your line of sight, like a clock at the front of the classroom. Without moving your eyes, take in anything that you can see to the left, to the right, above and below you. You can do this anytime your mind is racing, you're feeling overwhelmed, or need to take a break from staring at a computer screen!

COMMUNICATION + PERSONALITIES (aka HOW TO PLAY NICE WITH OTHERS)

~

★ First impressions

When someone meets you for the first time, it takes them about three seconds to make some sort of judgement about you—harsh but true! So the way you present yourself and communicate with a new person will have a lasting impact. It's also a chance to let your true self shine through.

Now I understand that meeting someone for the first time can be scary. What if they don't like you? What if you don't like them? What if you have nothing to talk about?

So first let me tell you that **most** people have these fears. But with one little switcheroo of a thought, you can shake that pressure off and actually enjoy the process. Are you ready for this mind-blowing, life-changing thought?

Answer this: If you walk into a room and you don't know anyone, then you walk out of that room without any new friends, what have you lost?

It's not a trick question. You don't need to try to outsmart me with answers like 'an opportunity.' You walk in with the same, usual friends. You walk out without any new ones. What have you lost? **Nothing!** (I may have exaggerated the 'mind-blowingness' of this but seriously, taking the pressure off yourself to ensure that everyone in the room likes you or you'll die can make the whole process so much more fun!)

So take the pressure off and be your beautiful self. And of course your nanna was right—use your lovely manners!

Nanna was right

Body language is everything when you meet someone for the first time. If I was to walk into a room where you and your friends were hanging out and I dragged my feet, looked like a mess, hadn't showered, looked down the whole time and kinda scowled at you, you'd probably think I was pretty weird.

So **how** you walk into a room says a lot about you. I know we shouldn't care about how we look but remember that 'first three seconds' rule? We can't get a lot of words out in that time, so we have to rely on the way we present ourselves.

It's not superficial to care about this stuff. How you present yourself to the world needs to align with who you are as a person. You're not trying to be someone that you're not here. And it's not only about **you** but more about how you make others feel. You're awesome and even though you and I know that, you've gotta give others a chance to see it.

So let's look at how we do that.

Posture

'Roll your shoulders back, Amanda!'

'Do you want to end up like the Hunchback of Notre Dame, Amanda?' (What even is that?)

'Stand up straight, Amanda!!'

'Don't slouch! (while actually physically grabbing my shoulders and rolling them back)

Clearly, this was an important topic for my father! So naturally, I hunched as much as possible throughout my teens, rolling my eyes every time Dad made a comment. :) Take that, Dad!

It wasn't until later in life that I realised how important it is to be mindful of my posture, particularly when I started seeing photos of myself in groups looking all hunched over! It's funny how it doesn't matter what our parents say, sometimes we just need to learn stuff for ourselves. (What do they know anyway, right?) But seriously, here's what you need to do . . .

Stand up tall (der)

To practise this, find a wall and stand with your back against it, making sure your heels, bottom and shoulders are against it as well. You need to roll your shoulders back, not lift them up towards your ears. And you want to engage your core muscles (think abs), so that you're supporting your spine and can lift up through the middle. Take in a couple of deep breaths against the wall and then step away. You may feel like you're pushing your boobs out at this point, but it only feels that way because you've been used to slouching. (I'm talking to you, tall drink of water!)

Be proud of who you are

Be open to new people, showing this through your body language. Keep your head up, smile (even if it feels a little forced—the act of smiling actually makes you feel great too), make eye contact with people and make an effort with your appearance (which we covered in the last section of the book).

Make eye contact

There's a little trick when it comes to making eye contact with people. I know it can feel a bit intense to look people in the eye sometimes. So next time you're with someone, try looking right between their eyebrows at what many spiritual practitioners call the 'wisdom eye.' When you do this, people will feel like you're looking into their eyes, even though you're not.

Shake hands

Yep. Stick with me here. I know it might feel like an 'old person' thing to do but it's such a great habit to get into. It instantly breaks down a barrier and shows confidence. It also avoids the awkward hug, kiss on the cheek, weird wave conundrum. You just take control, put your hand out and they will shake it. Trust me. You can practise your cool-girl-hand-through-the-hair manoeuvre if you want, just so you're prepared in case they are from Mars and don't know what a handshake is. But I've **never** had that happen to me, so you'll be fine.

Not to get too technical on you, but your handshake should include:

- A firm grip. You may feel like you're squeezing way too hard but right at the point where you feel like you could be crushing fingers is usually the perfect amount of pressure. Practise with your mum, sister, dad or bestie and see just how hard you can squeeze without causing pain. (But don't blame me if you are actually Superwoman and send a poor little girl to hospital!)

- Your thumbs should be interlocked and your fingers together. It's always your right hand that you offer, not your left.

Don't hesitate, just go for it! If this feels way too weird with your friends, keep this up your sleeve for job interviews or meeting adults like your parents' friends—they'll love it. I've had students get jobs **because of their handshake**. Seriously. They were turned away before they learnt this. But when they went back, introduced themselves with confidence, shook hands, made eye contact and smiled, they were offered a trial right there and then.

'In this day and age, young people just don't have the manners they used to,' said the old man in a croaky voice with terrible posture. You can break that stereotype with a simple handshake.

Introduce yourself

When introducing yourself, always include a greeting like 'hi' or 'hello' followed by your name (speaking as clearly as possible), then remember to repeat their name back to them. We often mumble our own name because we know it so well; so while it may seem obvs, saying your name clearly is really important. We then want to repeat their name back to them for a few reasons: to make sure we've got it right, to help us remember and because people like hearing their own name!

Ever struggled to remember someone's name? Here's another little trick: say it over in your head 3–5 times as soon as you hear it. If you do this, you'll lock it in. If you don't, you'll forget it a moment later and either start calling her 'babe' or 'mate' then have to admit you've already forgotten and ask her again.

Here's an example of a good intro:

Person 1: 'Hi, I'm Amanda.' *extends hand to shake*
Person 2: 'Hi Amanda, I'm Lauren. Nice to meet you.' *shakes hand*
Person 1: 'Nice to meet you too, Lauren.'

★ Body language

An extra note on body language: 50-80% of our communication is non-verbal. Our tone, the pitch of our voice, how we are standing, our gestures and expressions, our stance and proximity to the listener, how loud our voice is and our eye movements all contribute to how effectively we communicate.

Everyone can read body language intuitively, but it's important to remember that we all perceive things in different ways. So be mindful of how your body language might be perceived by others. For example, I might fold my arms across my chest because it makes me feel safe and comfortable. But another person might perceive that as me being closed off and stubborn. We're not mind-readers, so it's impossible to know how we're being perceived by others. But we can **be mindful**.

Typical body language cues:

- arms crossed—can mean closed off
- feet facing towards the door—can mean that we're trying to leave and don't want to be there
- feet facing towards the person we're in a conversation with—indicates we want to be there and are fully listening and engaged
- arms behind our back—can make others feel like we're hiding something
- arms by our side or loosely holding our hands in front of our body—usually a sign of open and trusting body language

- scratching the nose—can suggest we're not interested and are over the conversation (you're going to be so worried next time your nose is itchy—muhuhhahaha!) #evillaugh

Now all of these are just silly indicators and are not to be taken as absolute truth. But I always find it so interesting to learn more about how a simple movement can be interpreted by another person.

A quick way to make someone else feel comfortable is to mimic their body language. So if someone you're chatting with relaxes back in their chair and gets comfy, it can feel nice for them if you do the same. Or if someone leans forward on the table, you might do the same too. We actually tend to do this intuitively, without meaning to. Take notice next time you're chatting with someone and see if you end up copying what they do.

Side note: Body language affects how we feel too. If you study lying down on your bed, you won't get much done and won't take as much in, because your body is in relax mode. And if you stand up taller, lift your head and smile, you'll feel more confident. So fake it till you make it beautiful!

★ Power pose, baby

This research[22] by social psychologist and professor at Harvard Business School, Amy Cuddy, and her colleagues, will change your life. It's so simple and will help you to show up in a way that makes you **feel** more assertive, confident, optimistic, powerful and able to think on your feet, rather than feeling powerless.

---

22 Carney,D., Cuddy A., Yap, A. (2010) Power Posing, *Psychological Science* Vol 21, Issue 10, pp. 1363-68 http://faculty.haas.berkeley.edu/dana_carney/power.poses.PS.2010.pdf

It's called the **Power Pose**. All you do is stand tall with your feet shoulder width apart and hands either high in the air or on your hips, like Wonderwoman, for two minutes. Just two minutes! It causes a reaction to your testosterone and cortisol levels, making you feel more powerful and less stressed. Amazing, right?

Try using the Power Pose:

- before you have to speak at school (Go to the bathroom, lock yourself in a cubicle and do it.)
- before you go to a party that you're feeling a bit anxious about (Do it at home before you go.)
- before you have to ask your parents about something and want to make sure you show up confidently and share your best argument (Do this first for two minutes.)

You can watch the full TED Talk about this online. It's called: *Your body language may shape who you are.*

★ Making conversation

When we take away the fear of being liked by another person, getting to know a new person should be easy. After all, you don't know anything about them! It's interesting to learn about someone new, so ask open-ended questions, really listen and be engaged. Put your device down, make eye contact and keep an open posture.

Just ask questions and be interested in the answer. You'll be surprised at how effective this is. And remember, other people feel nervous meeting new people too. Be the brave one who opens up the conversation and asks questions.

Talking to adults

Adults generally love talking to young people. You make us feel young! And we love to feel needed and that you care about what we have to share. So asking us adults **anything** gets us all excited about sharing our eons of experience. So, don't ever be afraid. All the same tips above apply—introduce yourself and ask questions curiously and with respect.

Try this! ➤ Open-ended questions allow someone to give an answer that's longer than one or two words. A closed question is 'Did you have a good weekend?' because the answer is simply 'yes' or 'no.' An open-ended question would be 'What did you get up to this weekend?' Try it next time you're in a conversation with someone.

★ Words

Words having meaning and power, but only because we give them power.

We recently had a student share this example:

If a girl was to scream at you, 'You are such a **tree**!' would that upset you? Probably not, right? You might be confused but you probably wouldn't feel hurt the way another word would make you feel. (She used a few words as an example, but I'll let your imagination come up with something here to replace 'tree.')

The reason we don't feel much about that word is because there is no emotional charge added to it.

The moral of the story? If someone is calling you names, don't add the emotion—just pretend they are saying something like 'tree.' If you don't believe what they're saying, and I'm sure you know for certain that you're not a tree, then they can't hurt you. And on the flipside, realise how much power is in the words **you** choose. They can uplift someone, inspire thousands, motivate, serenade, belittle and hurt. So choose your own words carefully.

A few words or phrases to be mindful of:

- Swearing—it's just unnecessary most of the time and is harsh. To get a little woo-woo on you, using harsh language like that gives off a negative vibe, man. Plus if you never swear, then that one time you do will have a much bigger impact— think about that!

- Using the word 'actually' too much. For example: 'Actually, I believe that blah blah blah.' It shouldn't be a surprise to you that you have something to say or something to add to the conversation. Drop the 'actually' and own it! The same goes for words like 'literally' and 'honestly'—both are usually used to exaggerate something. For example, 'I like literally died.' (You didn't!) 'Honestly, what was she thinking?' (Aren't you always honest?) I'll admit, I've used a few of these words throughout the book . . . but not **all** the time.

- Using the word 'like' too much. For example, 'So, like, this happened, and I was like, so annoyed because, like, how dare they?' Just **why**? Totally unnecessary in that sentence and you come across as a bit of an airhead. #justsayin

- Saying 'I don't know' all the time, when you do know. It's just lazy and safe. Be brave and share your thoughts, opinions and wisdom with others. If you've got away with this in the past, you'll find that other people will jump in and answer for you so you never have to think. Not a great habit to get into.

- Adding 'just' to your sentences makes them less powerful. For example, 'I'm just worried that . . . ' sounds a little hesitant. Whereas 'I'm worried that . . . ' makes you sound much more sure of yourself.

★ Shine on social

There is nothing either good or bad,
but thinking makes it so.

William Shakespeare, English poet, playwright and actor

Many people think social media and technology in general are ruining our lives. That may be true but may be false. Like everything else in life, it's up to us to decide how we use it and how it makes us feel.

Most girls I speak to know how to protect themselves online. You get talks at school, at home and you watch out for each other too. So I'm not going to go into the details of that here. I'm more interested in making sure you feel great about yourself while using social media (because let's face it, you're always going to use it).

Some studies have shown that social media can have a positive impact on teen self-esteem[23,24,25]. However some research[26] suggests that the more time spent on social media,

---

23 Buchanan, B., Correlation between Facebook use and self esteem *Utah Valley University Thesis Collection* 2014

24 Gonzales AL., Hancock JT., Mirror, mirror on my Facebook wall: effects of exposure to Facebook on self-esteem, *Cyberpsychol Behav Soc Netw.* 2011 Jan-Feb; 14(1-2);79–83 doi: 10.1089/cyber.2009.0411

25 https://www.commonsensemedia.org/research/social-media-social-life-how-teens-view-their-digital-lives/key-finding-2%3A-teens-more-likely-to-report-positive-impact--

26 https://www.smh.com.au/technology/under-the-sway-of-social-media-20130720-2qaws.html#ixzz2al7asFuh

the more likely teens were to experience low self-esteem. Hmm confusing, right? With so much information out there, it's hard to know what's best but one thing many studies agree on is that self-esteem is affected by **how** social media sites are used.

Tips for shining on social

1. Make a choice to **use social media for good**. Find supportive, positive and inspiring people, create change and awareness campaigns, support each other and use it to connect with long-distance friends and family.
2. Don't post something that you wouldn't want your parents, nanna or a future boss to see.
3. Don't ever say something that you wouldn't feel comfortable saying to someone's face.
4. Don't air your dirty laundry on social media. If you're feeling really angry or upset, write in a journal instead.
5. Check in with how you're feeling as you scroll . . . Do you have a smile on your face or are you feeling withdrawn and closed off? I got a shock the other day while scrolling, when I accidently turned the camera on and it was facing me. My forehead was scrunched up as though I was really angry. It made me realise how important it is to check in with how you're feeling more often.
6. Set a timer on your phone before you start scrolling. An hour can go in the blink of an eye sometimes, so limit your scrolling to ten minutes (or whatever works for you) by setting a timer. You're a busy, shiny girl with stuff to do and places to be!
7. Make sure that, even if you make friends with people online, you still catch up with friends IRL. Nothing beats it.
8. Remember that you are amazing. You don't need 'likes' to tell you that.

9. Remember that up to 80% of communication is non-verbal and social media cuts out all of that! If you need to have an important conversation, then do it in person.

10. Don't spend excessive amounts of time being a 'passive follower.' Those who update their own profiles have higher self-esteem than those who simply scroll through other people's feeds. This doesn't mean you have to start posting more yourself (if you're not much of a sharer on social media that's great), but don't spend hours consuming other people's lives with mindless scrolling.

11. Create your own personal brand. Decide on the parts of your life you want to share online: do you want to share beauty or positivity or humour in the world and creatively express yourself that way online? Don't just share something for the sake of it—you never know how things can turn out. I know loads of social media 'influencers' who make money from their social media feeds. But a **lot of thought** goes into this and they curate their feed, consider what their 'audience' wants and **always** share something useful. Take charge of your feed and express your passions, purpose and joy through it.

12. And finally, remember that future employers will look you up, so don't share anything you might be embarrassed about later.

Did you know? ➤ Watching just three minutes of negative news in the morning can lead to a 27% increased chance of you having a bad day![27] So if you start the day scrolling through your feed and it makes you feel bad, is filled with

---

27 Harvard Business Review https://hbr.org/2015/09/
consuming-negative-news-can-make-you-less-effective-at-work

negative sob stories or so much unrealistic fitspo that you feel bad about yourself, then that will stick with you all day. Choose your feed and do things first thing in the morning that make you feel great! Watch a quick funny video while you're getting ready or put on your favourite song.

★ A note on making friends online

Despite the fear that this can bring up, I've actually made some of my best friends online. It's easy to find people who 'get' you, because you're sharing parts of yourself with the world in a way that feels good for you. It's easy to find people that love the same books as you, for example. But I only ever catch up with these beautiful friends for the first time in a group environment, like at an event that we're both interested in going to, and I always go with a friend/parent. It's just safer that way.

For you, I would say be extra careful. You might not think it's a big deal or that it happens in real life but there are lots of creeps in the world.

Can you believe this?!

One of our students, let's call her Jackie, made friends with someone online. It was a boy and he said all the right things. They spent hours online chatting with each other and she completely trusted him. Even though he said he lived in another city, she felt like he was becoming the love of her life. He listened. He asked the right questions and he was there for her. When he started sending her sexual messages, she felt she should respond, even though she didn't want to. So a whole role play happened. She didn't want to, but she liked this guy and didn't want to disappoint him. And she thought, what's the harm?

As Jackie walked into the school grounds the next day, she immediately knew that something was wrong. The boy turned out to be someone from her school and he had printed out the conversation and posted it on walls around the school. Can you believe that? Her parents got called in and they were devastated to see some of the language she had used. The boy was suspended and she felt awful about that too. But mostly she felt so betrayed. This person that she had trusted and shared her soul with had done something horrible.

The storm passed and no-one talks about it or cares about it anymore. So even if something crazy and embarrassing happens to you, it will get better. Jackie learnt who her real friends were and got through it.

So, please be super-duper careful with any of your dealings online. The above story actually has a bit of a 'happy ending' compared to the way some things end up online. More than a few girls have gone missing, thanks to online creeps. You have to be so careful.

Values + social media

Author and teen expert, Rebecca Sparrow, recommends that you get clear on your values **first** before posting online.[28] (See earlier advice in Part 1 about values.)

Rebecca also highlights a really important point: **happiness comes from in-person friendships and connections.** Online friends are more like your 'cheer squad' but they're not the ones you can count on when you really need a shoulder to cry on or someone to share birthday cake with. So it's important

---

28 Check out Rebecca's books and her work at http://rebeccasparrow.com/

to recognise this. They'll 'like' something (and we all need a bit of that 'like' love in our lives) but you need to cultivate **real friends** as well.

Try this! ➤ Mama Earth does so much for us, but did you know that being in nature actually clears your energy fields and can 'recharge' you?

So if you ever feel like the world is against you, or you need to be recharged, get outside among the trees, ocean, rivers, grass, sunshine and blue skies. Put down your device and plant your feet in Mother Nature.

★ Take shine-worthy action

Google yourself and have a look at your 'digital footprint' to see what you can find. Review your own social media channels. Are you expressing yourself authentically? Is that the 'real you' out there? Are you sharing positive, useful stuff with the world?

YOU VS THE WORLD—DIFFERENT PERSONALITIES

~

Want to know why some people make you tick and how you can best interact with others? Let's go!

There are loads of personality tests online and you've probably even had to do one at school. The cool thing about them is you get to know more about **you**. It's also pretty fun to start understanding why other people in your life seem crazy to you at times (don't worry, they think you're crazy sometimes too!).

I love a very simple personality-type model with four types: Powerful, Playful, Peaceful and Precise. I first heard about these four types through a woman I love and admire, Kim Morrison. But this stuff is **ancient**. It originally came from the work of Hippocrates over 2000 years ago and is one of the oldest personality-type systems in the world. You'll see from understanding more about each type that, as Kim would say: 'We're all just different—not wrong!' Understanding this stuff helps you realise that no-one is out to get you and that there's a reason we get along with some people and not with others. It's human nature.

Note: As we learned earlier in the book, your personality isn't completely set in stone and we can change the way we think and feel. So use this as a fun guide, but don't get too caught up in your type—you'll naturally display traits from all four types but will notice that you're dominant in one or two of them.

★ Where did the idea of personality types come from?

At the heart of the four temperaments model is an ancient medical concept: humorism. Humors here refer to bodily fluids that are present within the body. Different people have different proportions of these fluids; the predominance of one fluid defines a person's temperament and psychological type.[29]

The four temperaments and their predominant humors (bodily fluids) are:

1. Sanguine: blood
2. Phlegmatic: phlegm
3. Choleric: yellow bile
4. Melancholic: black bile

The predominance of one humor was said to affect one's appearance and behaviour.

The concept has become popular again in recent decades and two experts in the field, Allison Mooney and Kim Morrison[30] talk about personality types like this:

• Powerful Choleric
• Playful Sanguine
• Peaceful Phlegmatic
• Precise Melancholic

So . . . are you Powerful, Playful, Peaceful or Precise?

---

29 The World of Shakespeare's Humors, History of Medicine. *U.S. National Library of Medicine.* https://www.nlm.nih.gov/exhibition/shakespeare/fourhumors.html
30 Morrison, K. *Why Can't You Be Normal Like Me?* eBook http://twenty8.com

★ The Powerful Type

The Powerful are:

- doers
- love to lead
- decisive and strong willed
- would be the director of a play
- 'Let's do it **my** way!'

Powerful Penny is the leader of the group. She'll take charge and make decisions. If you need something done, you know you can ask her and she'll get it done (or get someone else to do it!).

Powerful Penny is ambitious and goal driven. She's not afraid of confrontation and you can feel her presence in a room. She can bring change and get stuff done, so can also be restless and impatient. She needs credit for her accomplishments, loyalty and appreciation for what she does. When stressed, Powerful Penny will work harder, try to get a tighter grip on control, may exercise more and can get angry.

★ The Playful Type

The Playful are:

- talkers
- enthusiastic + funny
- outgoing and love to tell stories
- would be the actor in a play
- 'Let's do it the **fun** way!'

Playful Sally gets into trouble at school for being disruptive. When she tells a story everyone listens, but you just know she's going to exaggerate! Sally will forgive you quickly and just wants to get back to having fun. She makes you feel good.

Playful Sally needs attention, affection, acceptance and may be messy and easily distracted! She's highly motivated, loves to be in groups, is enthusiastic and very charming. When she's stressed she might go shopping, throw a tantrum, talks more or needs to leave the scene.

★ The Peaceful Type

The Peaceful are:

- watchers (not in a creepy way)
- diplomatic + patient
- would be the audience at a play
- 'Let's do it the **easy** way!'

Peaceful Polly doesn't like to feel overwhelmed. You feel calm in her presence and you feel like she really listens to you. She might seem lazy at times but she's just conserving her energy!

Peaceful Polly needs peace and quiet, respect and to be valued. Oh, and she doesn't mind procrastinating! She can also be stubborn, even though she seems so gentle. She's easygoing, warm, and very people-oriented. She's adaptable, balanced and seeks harmony. When stressed, she tends to disconnect, watch TV, shuts down and sleeps.

★ The Precise Type

The Precise are:

- thinkers
- detail-oriented
- would be the producer in a play
- 'Let's do it the **right** way!'

Precise Pamela does things right and has high standards. She loves lists, analyses everything and always looks polished. She loves to learn, has integrity and is a great planner.

Precise Pamela needs space, sensitivity and support. She can give the silent treatment and be moody when upset and hates mistakes. When stressed, she can get lost in a book or TV, criticises, becomes judgemental or can give up.

The purpose of these types is to understand more about who you are so you can **embrace** that. If you're a precise personality type, then plan little day trips with your friends, print out beautiful itineraries for everyone and enjoy that side of you! If you're peaceful (like I am), then recognise that you need to be quite disciplined with yourself to get stuff done and give yourself time in your day/week to have quiet time to meditate, walk, nap–whatever you need to recharge. If you're playful, then embrace that about yourself–be playful, tell stories and find ways to express yourself. If you're powerful, take charge and set goals for yourself. Find ways to put your skills and natural personality traits to good use!

★ Connecting with different types

We're often attracted to people who have the opposite personality type to us. We are drawn to them because we wish we could be more like them and are fascinated by how they do things or because we feel balanced by being in their presence.

Powerful people feel calm when they're with Peaceful people and Peaceful people love that they can just go with the flow, while the Powerful people make all the decisions! Precise people love how Playful people can be the life of the party and be so spontaneous, while Playful people love how detailed and specific Precise people are. Note: This is also why we can clash with people!

★ Communicating with other types

If we understand how others are, then we can communicate with them in a way that they will understand. For example, if you have a Precise parent, then give them as many facts and important details as you can (write out a list and leave it on the kitchen bench–they'll love it). Let them know exactly where you'll be, what time you'll call them and don't be late! If you have a Playful friend, share a story with her (rather than all the facts), surprise her with a spontaneous adventure and call her to ask her all about her day (they don't mind talking about themselves!). If you upset a Precise friend, realise that it's going to take a bit of time for them to get over it and give them space. If you have a Peaceful sister, realise that she might need a bit more downtime on her own. It doesn't mean she doesn't love you. When communicating with her, let her know how you feel about something and then give her time to process before she comes back to you.

For more information about these types, check out Kim Morrison's ebook: *Why Can't You Be Normal Like Me?*

★ Take shine-worthy action

Which personality type are you? Write down which one you think you are and what you think the people in your family would be.

....

....

....

....

Extra Info! ➤ Do you know where you sit on the extrovert-introvert spectrum? Extroverted people are typically more outgoing and introverted people are considered quieter. One of our favourite introverted psychologists, Thania Siauw, shared this with us:

> *We live in a culture that seems to favour extroverted qualities over introverted traits. This can mean that introverts, 50% of our population, can be left feeling like they are misunderstood, or not as valued in our society.*

It is often the misconception that introverts are 'shy' people when in fact, many are not—it is more that they have a preference over what context they relate to people in. Introverts can even be perceived as not liking other people, which is also not true.

Research shows that the brains of introverts and extroverts are quite different in regard to how they respond to stimuli, including social stimuli.[31] One of the main differences is that introverts are energised from spending time alone, while extroverts recharge from the energy of other people. This has a lot to do with feel-good neurotransmitters in our brain. Introverts like to use acetylcholine, a neurotransmitter which makes calm environments and going inwards (rather than focusing outwards) feel pleasurable.[32] Whereas, extraverts respond more to dopamine, which is a chemical in the brain that provides the motivation to seek external rewards like

---

31 Fishman I, Ng R, Bellugi U. Do extraverts process social stimuli differently from introverts? *Cognitive neuroscience*. 2011;2(2):67–73. doi:10.1080/17588928.2010.5274 34.

32 Fonseca, C. (2013) *Quiet Kids: Help Your Introverted Child Succeed in an Extraverted World*. Prufrock Press: Texas.

earning money, climbing the social ladder, etc.[33] Extroverts and introverts have both of these chemicals in the brain, they just process a little differently depending on where you are on the spectrum.

It can be useful to understand this and be aware of what helps to energise you, as a way of understanding **you**, instead of putting pressure on yourself to perhaps do what you think is expected of you. Sometimes you may not feel like going to that party or joining in on every conversation around you, and you may need to spend time recouping after a social situation—that is totally okay and normal for many people! Alternatively, you may need to study with others or go out with your friends to fill up your tank.

★ When your parents just don't get it

Ahh, parents! They were our heroes growing up and we thought they knew everything there is to know in the world. Now there might be times when they drive you up the wall. But if you think about it, they are always doing the best they can, with the knowledge they have.

A few things to keep in mind for building a strong relationship with your parents:

- They love you. Yep. Your parents love you. Sooooooo much.
- Unless you've got 73 siblings (seems impossible) then remember that your parents are learning too. Most haven't

---

33 Granneman, J. *The Scientific Resasons Why Introverts and Extroverts Are Different.* Huffington Post. https://www.huffingtonpost.com/entry/the-scientific-reasons-why-introverts-and-extroverts-are-different_us_566eedf6e4b011b83a6be33a (last accessed 18 May 2018)

been a parent to a child your age or have only done it once or twice with your older siblings. And I'm sure if you think about your older siblings, you'll agree that you're pretty different to them. Your parents are learning how to parent you as they go along. Cut them some slack every once in a while.

- Help them to help you. You need to find a way to communicate with your parents. If you can tell them how you're feeling, let them know what you need from them, share what's going on in your life with them and **trust** them, then you'll have much more chance of them trusting you too. It's a two-way street. If you struggle to speak to them face-to-face, then write them letters, send them texts, talk to them while they tuck you in at night (you still get bedtime stories, right?) or leave them lovely long voice messages.

- Help them out. I know it can seem like magical fairies wash your clothes each week, but those fairies don't exist. It's usually someone pretty amazing in your household. So help them out. If you're hoping your parents will notice that you're becoming a mature adult (let's face it, you want to go out and have a bit of freedom, right?), then you need to show them that you're a responsible person.

- Tell them that you love them. Every chance you get.

Hold on my darling. This feels like everything right now but the best stuff is waiting for you—richer love, deeper friendship and adventures that will make your soul somersault. And listen to your mum—she's right about most things and one day will be the love of your life.

Nina Tovey, director of Yoke Communications,
on what she'd share with her teen self

HOW TO GET EVERYTHING YOU WANT IN LIFE (aka MANNERS)

*Friends and good manners will carry
you where money won't go.*

Margaret Walker, American poet and writer

★ Modern manners 101

We've all had experiences where someone has just been kind of a jerk or impolite. It's not nice. On the flipside, I've seen how using some basic manners can help you get pretty much anything you want. In a world where there are more than a few jerks around, being the polite one gets you places. #goingplaceswithasmile

✓ **Please and thankyou.** It's so simple. Saying 'please' and a heartfelt 'thankyou,' even to the bus driver as you get off the bus, is a lovely little gift of gratitude you can share with others.

✓ **Ask nicely.** You'll be surprised by what people will agree to and will do for you if you ask nicely. This includes doing it without expectation . . . ask the question but be okay if the answer is 'no.' In fact, you can say that too: 'I was wondering if [insert what you'd love help with here] but totally okay if you can't do that, just thought I'd ask.' As soon as the other person feels like it's their choice and you're not trying to manipulate them, they'll be much more open to saying 'yes.'

✓ **Open the door for others.** It doesn't have to be a thing that men do for women only. Let's change the status quo and open the door for other people.

✓ **People love to hear their names.** So use them in conversation.

✓ **Table etiquette.** See below for all the tips you need to feel comfortable at a fancy restaurant or first date!

✓ **Get up for old people.** If you're on public transport and see someone elderly get on, make sure you get up for them so they can sit down. Do this in everyday life too—be on the lookout for ways you can help someone. If you see an elderly person struggling with their trolley at the supermarket, ask if they'd like some help. Too often, people see a problem and don't do anything to help. The elderly person might say 'no' and that's okay too. At least you offered. Note: Even though I just said 'elderly' three times, you can help anyone!

✓ **Remember all the other things** we've discussed in this book: present yourself nicely, introduce yourself, ask questions, focus and listen to people.

★ Table etiquette

Ever felt uncomfortable at the dinner table? It's not a nice feeling when you're not sure which fork to pick up while at a wedding or your formal. I want you to enjoy yourself, so let's dive in!

Good table manners start at home—try to eat at the dinner table regularly and use that time to find out a bit more about the people around you. Ask how your mum or dad's day was—they'll really appreciate it and you just might find out something new and interesting. Believe it or not, they actually had lives before you came along!

✶ Dining Options

Set menu

This is when the menu has been prearranged, so the cutlery will already be laid out in front of you. This is common for large functions such as weddings, formals, awards nights, etc.

While the menu has already been decided, you will usually have a couple of options and these will be alternatively served around the table, eg. you may be served chicken and your neighbour served fish and this pattern will continue around the table. If you have any special dietary requirements, you'll need to notify the restaurant, function venue or host prior to the night.

Table d'hôte

This literally means 'host's table' in French and indicates a menu where multiple courses are offered at a fixed price, eg. five courses for $69.95.

À la carte

This is when you simply order from the menu. Most restaurants and cafes would be considered à la carte. The appropriate cutlery will be set after you place your order.

Buffet

This is when you pay a set price for 'all you can eat.' A variety of food is usually on display and you get up from your table and help yourself to as many courses as you wish. There is no need to overload your plate, as you can go back for more if you wish. You will normally have to collect your cutlery as well.

Hors d'oeuvres

Also known as appetisers or finger food, hors d'oeuvres are usually served while guests are standing at functions or parties. Make sure you take a napkin from the tray or service person and find a bin to discard anything you don't eat (rather than putting a toothpick or any scraps back on the tray).

Tapas

A tapas menu will offer a variety of small dishes for you to select and share among your table.

★ Fine dining

In a fine dining restaurant, the first thing that will happen once your waiter has shown you to your table is that they will pull your chair out for you. Stand in front of the chair and, once you feel the chair touching the back of your knees, start to sit and pull the chair in yourself. Once you are seated, the waiter will stand to your right and drop the napkin on your lap. No matter what kind of restaurant or café you're in, you should always place the napkin, even a paper one, in your lap (yes, even if you're at McDonalds).

Always wait for your host or hostess to lift their fork before you start eating.

★ Cutlery and crockery

- With your cutlery, always work from the outside in. The first set of cutlery you will use is smallest fork on the far left and smallest knife or spoon on the far right.

- Forks are usually on the left and knives and spoons on the right. One exception is when pasta is served–then the fork will be on the right and a spoon on the left.
- Your glass will be above the main knife, top right from your main plate.
- Your bread plate will always be on the left of your main plate.
- The resting positions of your cutlery communicate to the service staff whether you are still eating or have finished your meal. Place your knife and fork together in the middle of your plate, when you have finished your meal.

★ Table Manners

- It's polite to wait until everyone has their meal before you begin to eat.
- Only take small bite-sized pieces.
- If you're pouring yourself a drink, offer one to the people around you, or just fill up their water glass if you can see it is empty.
- Always bring your food to your mouth, not your mouth to your food. If you're sitting up straight with your napkin in your lap, any food that spills should fall straight into the napkin.
- If you cannot eat something, bring your napkin up to your mouth and discreetly spit it into your napkin. Ask the waiter for a new napkin–politely of course, no whistling or clicking your fingers at them!
- When eating soup, always scoop the spoon away from you. When you get near the bottom, tip the bowl slightly away from you to scoop up the rest. Use your spoon to pour the soup into your mouth, rather than slurp it off the spoon. If the soup is too hot, start at the outer edges of the soup, as the middle will always be the hottest part.

- Always excuse yourself if you need to leave the table during a meal. Place your napkin on the back or arm of the chair, then back in your lap when you return.
- Don't speak with your mouth full. If you have nearly finished chewing, place your hand in front of your mouth as you speak. No-one wants to see what's going on in there!
- If you are using your fingers to eat food such as chips or pizza, wipe your fingers on your napkin rather than lick them.
- Keep your handbag and mobile phone off the table. Place it on the floor under your chair or somewhere else out of the way.
- Keep your elbows off the table during the main meal. You can relax a bit more once everything has been cleared from the table.
- Do not reach across the table or across your neighbour to grab at something; ask for it to be passed to you.
- Do not do any grooming at the table. Excuse yourself and go to the bathroom if you need to apply make-up, comb your hair, etc.
- If you are someone who talks with big hand gestures, make sure you put your cutlery down before you start waving your hands around, or you may take out someone's eye!

Most importantly, relax and enjoy the ritual of sharing a meal with others.

FRIENDSHIPS

~

Spread love everywhere you go, let no-one ever come
to you without leaving happier.

Mother Teresa, humanitarian and Catholic saint

★ How to make friends

People come into our lives as friends in three ways: for a reason, a season or a lifetime.

It's important to understand that not everyone is going to be a **lifetime** friend and that's okay. Those friends are rare. They are the ones who are there for you always and who you feel really, truly get you. They understand you. You would drop anything to help them and vice versa. Hopefully they'll be in your life for a lifetime, even if you have spells when you don't see much of each other.

Other friends are there for a **reason**—they come into your life because you need to learn something from them or they need to learn something from you. Once that reason is over, you tend to drift apart and that's okay.

And others are there for a **season**—often by circumstance. These might be the majority of your schoolfriends, people you work with or maybe the girls on your netball or football team. You might not have loads in common with these friends but you get along okay and can make the most of these friendships while they're there. You probably wouldn't share your deepest secrets with them though.

Lifetime friends **will** come into your life. If you haven't found any yet, that's okay. You will. Be open to these ones looking or acting a little differently too. You see it in movies all the time— it's often the unlikely couple who end up having the most fun together and being good friends for a lifetime. And even if your BFF hasn't shown up yet, that doesn't mean you can't make an effort with your 'reason' and 'season' friends. We all need company and we all give each other different things.

We deepen our friendships by **caring for one another** and opening up about what's going on for us.

> *That friend who loves you is the one who*
> *doesn't judge you, not the coolest one!*
>
> Libby Schuring, teacher and youth mentor, on
> what she would share with her teen self

IRL → What if your friend tells you she's thinking about committing suicide? I've heard this a few times over the last couple of years and it causes so much stress for the friend who hears it.

Here's what you need to do:

- Stay on the phone or with your friend if you can. Don't leave them alone.
- Tell an adult straightaway, even if your friend asks you not to. It's not fair for them to tell you something so serious

and ask you to keep it a secret. You can't risk something happening to them so **tell an adult**, either your own parents or even the girl's parents if you can. Even if your friend hates you for a while, at least you know you've done the right thing.

- Ask them if they have a plan. If they have a thought-out plan then they are at greater risk of doing something. If you think, even for a moment, that they're going to do something now, call the emergency number for police or ambulance straightaway. Police actually spend a lot of their time helping people in trouble like this, so don't ever be afraid to do this.
- Call Kid's Helpline if you need to. They're great at talking you through what to do.
- You should never have to deal with this on your own.

★ #Squadgoals

What do you see when you look at your current group of friends or 'squad'? Are they there for each other, kind and fun people to hang out with, or are they constantly complaining, whining and bitching?

It's hard to feel happy and confident if the people around you are constantly being negative. Surrounding yourself with happy, positive people can give you the strength and support to be your happy self and give things a go.

But it goes both ways. Like attracts like. We attract people into our life who treat us the way we treat ourselves. Take a moment to think about the people in your life and remember the exercise we did earlier in the book (thinking of the top five people we hang out with).

If you hang out with people who gossip and criticise all day long, you will most likely start criticising people yourself. If you hang out with kind, giving people, you will generally be more kind and giving yourself. It can be hard to change your group of friends when you are all at school together, but why not try to lead by example and be the person you want to be, even if that's a little different to your friends. They might follow your example.

Here are some tips for strong friendships:

Be vulnerable

In our courses, we sometimes do an icebreaker called 'If you really knew me.' We get into pairs and, even though the girls have only known each other for a day or so, they go and sit somewhere quiet and start a sentence with: 'If you really knew me . . . ' then proceed to share something personal. The other person just sits there listening, without needing to respond, fix or comfort the other person. Just listening. Then they swap.

It's a beautiful thing to do because they instantly become closer and realise that we **all** have stuff going on in our lives and we're all just trying to do our best at this thing called life. So even though it feels scary, don't be afraid to trust someone and open up (not everyone, but **someone**).

> *Beautiful girl, know that you are enough. Some of the most important relationships in your life now are still just as important in twenty years' time. Don't be afraid to nurture them **your** way. Your tears are beautiful and valid and they will cleanse you more than you know. You have everything you need darling girl, the key lies in realising that.*
>
> Emma Newby, photographer, life coach and youth mentor, sharing what she would tell her teen self

Ask for what you need + be strong

Practise being a good communicator and a good friend. And even say to your friends, 'You know what, I need to just talk something out. I don't need you to give advice or say anything, but I just need you to listen. Is that okay?' Let them know what you need from them—it makes life easier for them too!

You're only a victim in a relationship or friendship if you allow yourself to be. So don't give your power away. No-one can make you feel a certain way. While we can't control what others do or say, we can control how we react.

Don't gossip

If your friends gossip and bitch behind other people's backs to you, you can be fairly sure they are doing the same thing about you to others.

You don't ever have to argue with them or pull them up on it, if you don't want to. But you don't have to participate in it. If you start being kinder to people, maybe they will be kinder too. Change the subject. Gossip can seem harmless but I have seen, even in adults, how it can ruin families and friendships and get people in a crazy amount of trouble, when rumours that aren't true are spread around. It's serious business; don't do it.

Here's a brilliant saying: *Great minds discuss ideas, average minds discuss events, small minds discuss people.*

★ Take shine-worthy action

Try changing the subject next time someone is bitching or gossiping.

★ Bullying

Don't be afraid to speak up or to ask for help. Don't let anyone tell you to be quiet. Don't go silent on what matters or what affects you. It's brave to speak your truth and to ask for help when you need it. There is always someone who will support you.

Sharyn Holmes, founder of *Gutsy Girls Will Rule the World* on what she'd share with her teen self

Bullying has always been around. There is always someone who doesn't feel very good about themselves and so puts others down to feel better. The thing is, they don't actually feel better but they don't know what else to do. They might have a parent at home who bullies them and they don't know any better.

The difference these days is that it can now happen online, which is even more cowardly. It takes a very sad person to send hurtful messages to someone online, post rude comments or participate in any sort of online abuse.

If you see something upsetting, try to step away from the computer or turn off your phone for a while. Don't respond straightaway or forward the message to someone else in the heat of the moment. Find something to distract you from what's going on. Do something you love that doesn't give you time to think about what's happening, like playing the guitar, going for a run, or immersing yourself in a book or movie. You can also just chat with a parent, sibling or pet (animals are **the best** listeners).

Taking a break allows you to keep things in perspective and focus on the good things in your life. It also gives you time to figure out how you want to handle the situation.

If you are being bullied, make sure you tell someone, even if it's not straightaway. If someone is bullying you, then they will be bullying others too. Don't let those others suffer in silence.

Resist the urge to retaliate or respond

Walking away or taking a break when you're faced with online bullying also gives you some space, so you won't be tempted to fire back a response or engage with the bully or bullies. Responding when we're upset can make things worse. (Standing up to a bully can be effective sometimes, but it's more likely to provoke that person and escalate the situation.)

Taking a break gives the power back to you! Think about this: if you are walking along the street and a dog barks at you, do you turn around, get down on your hands and knees and start barking back at the dog? Probably not. Because you're not a dog. Same goes for bullying–**don't reduce yourself to their level**.

Be safe online

Password protect your phone and your online sites, and change your passwords often. Be sure to share your passwords only with your parent or guardian. Think twice before sharing personal information or photos/videos that you don't want the whole world to see. Once you've posted a photo or message, it can be difficult or impossible to delete it. So be cautious when posting photos or responding to someone's upsetting message.

> *Your truth is within you. When you follow this you will find your true friends and meaning. If it doesn't feel right, don't change yourself because it's obviously not your truth.*
>
> Leah Castle, founder of *Sharing Our Unique Lives* on what she'd share with her teen self

★ Boys + girls

Romantic love (regardless of gender) could fill a book all on its own. But there are a few things I want to make absolutely clear to you right here and now:

1. You will find love. If not now, then one day.
2. Start by loving yourself—that's how you attract the perfect person into your life. (Refer to almost every other section in this book on how to fall in love with yourself.)
3. Don't settle. If someone is treating you in a way that doesn't feel right for you, then leave. And if that's challenging for you, ask for help. If you're scared in any way by your partner, then you need to ask for help.
4. You will feel heartache at some stage in your life. It will be so intense that you'll feel like you could never be happy again. It will be gut-wrenching, life-is-not-worth-living intense. And then it gets a little bit easier. And eventually, you are like 'Why was I so hung up on that person?' So keep going. Do little things to treat yourself during this time. Reconnect with friends who love you and be gentle with yourself. Don't go calling the ex or texting them in the middle of the night and don't go stalking them on social media. You're stronger than that!
5. Sometimes it's just not quite the right time. My partner and I have been together for over ten years and he's awesome. But we were friends for years first. And then we broke up in there at some stage too. It was meant to be, so we found our way back to each other. Trust in life and love and you can't go wrong.

Your friends will most likely still be your friends in ten years. The same cannot be said for your boyfriend. Invest your time and your heart wisely. Do not make decisions based upon what other people might think. Make decisions based upon what you know to be true.

Sally Mills-Murray, one of my best friends from
school on what she'd share with her teen self

★ What to do when everything goes wrong

You are so smart, so beautiful, and capable of more than you realise. The struggles you're facing now will fade and one day they will be your greatest strength. You are loved by so many people.

Fiona Cameron, youth mentor, on what she
would share with her teen self

As much as I would love to tell you that life is always magical if you just believe it will be, that's not really how things work. Life can change in an instant.

So what do you do if you're smack bang in the middle of a crisis? Check in with yourself and ask yourself these questions:

- Is this really, honestly, as bad as it feels or as bad as I'm making out?
- What actually happened? (List out the facts.)
- How has this affected me? (Using 'I' language, write down how you are feeling: 'I feel hurt because . . . ')
- What can I do to feel better right now? (This could be as simple as a shower or bath. Check your building blocks to shine or self-care menu from pages 66,67 or 109.)
- Is there something I should do to fix the situation? And if so, what can I do?

Stay strong little one, everything will be okay.

Alisha Coon, former dancer and founder of *Self*
Savvi on what she'd share with her teen self

Sometimes we blow things out of proportion in our minds and dramatise things. That's okay, but if you can get clear on what has happened using the above questions, it will **help you to get perspective** and start dealing with the situation.

Keep smiling and always be love. The growth
and challenges you will face will become
your biggest blessings . . . you'll see.

Joanne Dawe, co-founder of *Grateful for Me* on
what she'd share with her teen self

SO, WHAT DO YOU WANT TO BE WHEN YOU GET OLDER?

This could possibly be the worst question of all time, right? The amount of stress it causes for teens is on par with flunking out of school for real.

One of my favourite songs, that I think you might like too, is *Amazing Life* by Clare Bowditch. It starts off like this:

You want to write a novel, make beautiful music
Act in the theatre with inspiring humans,
Learn a language
Run like the wind and help people fit in.
Travel to every country, make a million dollars
Smile when your children have babies
Make the heart your home, inviting and warm.

You want an amazing life, but you can't decide.
You think you have to be fully formed already,
    don't you?

You want an amazing life, but you can't decide.
You don't have to be just one thing,
But you have to start with something.

I know so many women in their twenties and thirties who still feel paralysed by the thought of choosing the one thing they are born to do. Finding their purpose. Figuring out their career and then getting started, all the while feeling like time is rushing by and if they don't get started soon, then they'll somehow be 'behind.'

So let me make it clear to you right here and now: **you do not need to have it all figured out.**

And if you have no idea what you want to be, start with what you don't want to be. This is what a pretty cool guy, Josh Shipp, suggests in his book *The Teen's Guide to World Domination*. If you know for sure that you don't want to collect garbage, sing on stage or be a firefighter, then you are a little closer to what you **do** want to do as a career.

You don't need to prove your worth.
You are already worthy.

Diana Braybrooke, teacher and anxiety coach
on what she'd share with her teen self

★ Get comfortable being uncomfortable

I'll tell you a secret: no-one has it all figured out. We're all finding our way in life and when we think we have it all figured out, a new problem or issue emerges for us to deal with. In the business world they say 'new level, new devil' because as you continue to grow your business, you feel a new sense of nervousness and have new challenges. It never ends. So the sooner you feel comfortable about being uncomfortable, the more growth and fun experiences you'll have in life.

★ Finding your purpose

Focus on what you love and let your heart guide you.

Michelle Marie McGrath, self-love mentor, on
what she'd share with her teen self

Some people know, with all of their being, what they are here to do. They have a passion and have always known it. Writer Elizabeth Gilbert is like that and she explains that these people are like jackhammers—they have always known what they are here to do and they just drill down, getting lots done and being super focused. Whereas other people, and I'm one of them, are hummingbirds. Hummingbirds flutter around from here to here to here, cross-pollinating, trying different things. Hummingbirds can feel anxious about this, because in our society it's revered to have found your burning desire to do this one thing you're born to do.[34]

But we don't all wake up knowing what we're born to do. If you think you might be a hummingbird, never fear. They create incredibly rich, complex lives for themselves. They bring an idea from here, to here, to here and we need that. If something feels right, keep doing it. If you're doing something and it doesn't feel right anymore, move on. Release yourself from the pressure and anxiety, and humbly and faithfully choose to continue to follow the hummingbird path.

As Gilbert says: *If you do that you might just look up and realise that you are exactly where you are meant to be.*

My one piece of advice to the hummingbirds would be to **pick one thing** and start with that. If you need to change later, that's okay. But don't get stuck not doing anything because you

---

34 Watch the video of Elizabeth Gilbert speaking about this on Oprah's SuperSoul
   Conversations here: http://www.oprah.com/own-supersoulsessions/elizabeth-gilbert-
   the-curiosity-driven-life-video (last accessed 18 May 2018)

can't decide. It's not the end of the world if you change later. These days, people stay in one career for about seven years before they move on anyway, hummingbird or not!

And if you're a jackhammer, be who you were born to be **now.** If you want to be a writer, be a writer. If you want to be a comedian, start working on your content now and be a comedian. Want to be your own boss? Start researching business courses online and play around with how you can start a business right now. This time of your life is a great time to start exploring and trying things out!

★ Do the hard things sometimes

Regardless of what you decide to do with your life, it's not always going to be easy. No matter what. At some stage, you'll have to do things you don't necessarily want to do, in order to get to where you want to go. Be prepared for this and don't shy away from a bit of hard, passionate work.

There's never a perfect time to get started on your dreams. This is something most adults still don't quite get. They don't fulfil their potential and have a million excuses why that didn't happen. Don't be that person. It's not always easy to follow your passion (or curiosity for the hummingbirds!) and do what feels right for you. When you take the leap and give it a go though, it's **oh so worth it.**

★ Get an idea of what you might like to do

*If you do work you love, and the work
fulfils you, the rest will come.*

Oprah Winfrey, American talk show host

Let's look past the school subjects you're good at for a moment, and get an idea of what would really, truly light you up. Because one thing I know for sure is that **you can enjoy your work**.

I had a student's mum say recently that her daughter loves make-up (and she's **great** at it, I've seen her!) but she said: 'There's not much money in make-up, so she shouldn't do it.' This just isn't true. Sometimes parents have a very clear vision of what they'd like their kids to do and, because they love you so so much, they get scared and worried that you'll end up heading down the 'wrong path.'

But if you do what you **love**, you can't go wrong. I know make-up artists who make well over $100,000 a year. Because they love it, they're great at it. They might travel the world doing fashion make-up or live in an exotic destination and just get booked out all year doing bridal make-up. There are so many ways to make money these days and if you present yourself well, are professional, do the work and embrace your own strengths and passions you can't go wrong.

Follow the joy

Just because you're good at accounting and accountants make a decent salary, that doesn't mean you want to sit in an office all day and crunch numbers. There has to be a balance between your passions, the way you want to live, the causes you feel strongly about, the person you want to be, your personality, your skills and your **joy**.

Try it on

According to psychologist, Christina Leggett, the teen years 'are often the best time to action ideas, learn new skills, write, create, draw and experiment with your identity (in safe ways of course).'[35] Even if it's scary to start something new, especially if your friends aren't into it, it's important to remember that we're multi-faceted and have so many parts to us. We can be into soccer **and** also really into illustrating or want to go and do a make-up course on the weekends. Christina says: 'It's about not being too rigid with concepts, and about exploring and learning with an open mind.'

★ Take shine-worthy action

Get clear on what you love by answering the following questions:

- What do you love doing?
- Look back at your list of values and strengths. How could they serve you in your work?
- What do your friends ask you for advice about?
- What can you do for hours without even noticing the time?
- What upsets you about the world? Where would you like to make a change? (This can lead you down a path of working in an area that feels of service, such as human rights.)

Visualise yourself in ten years' time . . . Get your journal or notebook, close your eyes take a few deep breaths and have a think about it. What's around you? What do you do when you wake up? What do you eat for breakfast? Where do you go for work? What's the structure of your day like? Who are you serving or helping? Scribble it all down and see what comes up for you. I've created an audio for you to download guiding you through this at www.shinefromwithinhq.com

---

35 Siauw, T and Leggett, C. "Module 2, Video 5: Guest teacher interview with psychologists." *Youth Mentor Training,* by Shine From Within, 2016.

★ Fund your fun now

If you're approaching (or have long passed) the age of being able to get a job, and you don't have one yet, you probably sit in one of two camps:

1. You dread the thought of getting a job and are so freaked out about the thought that you're coming up with excuses left and right to avoid it.
2. You can't **wait** to get a job—hello freedom and money!

For those who are dreading it, find a way to move through it. Get comfortable feeling uncomfortable! Everyone has a first job and everyone is totally freaked out about the thought of starting something new. I get it—it's a new team of people, new processes and procedures to learn and new opportunities to potentially fail. And if you're feeling scared about it, you absolutely have to find a way to move through it.

That's how you learn to get over your fears. Feeling the fear and then **doing it anyway.** Fear comes up in all sorts of situations, it's up to you to decide how you deal with it. I can guarantee you that you will feel more confident in yourself once you're settled in, have your own work crew and are bringing in the big bucks.

If you're ready and pumped to get out there, then you just need to find a job! Here are the common places you can search to find one:

- newspaper
- noticeboards
- chatting with friends
- careers websites
- work experience or internships
- connecting with potential employers through social media sites like LinkedIn.com

*Do what you love and that which
brings a smile to your face!*

Gabrielle Goldklang, youth mentor and founder of
Girl Wisdom on what she'd tell her teen self

★ The application

Create a one or two-page résumé with your contact details, experiences and skills. Make sure you include a photo of yourself at the top (not a selfie with your friends but a headshot of you against a white wall, looking semi-professional with a friendly smile). Include a cover letter or a paragraph at the top of your résumé, explaining why you want to work in that particular place.

You should also include two references. These are adults that the employers can call to ask about what you're like. It can't be your family, so someone like a teacher at school, netball coach, previous employer or neighbour would be great. You usually just include their name, title and phone number.

Follow up!

One of the biggest mistakes that we can make when applying for a job is failing to follow up. Always follow up an application with a phone call, or drop in to ensure your application has been received and you are top of mind. This will show that you are proactive and very interested in the role.

Telephone manner

Your telephone manner is very important, regardless of the type of job that you are applying for:

- Smile when on the phone—you can hear the smile in your voice.

- Don't mumble and make sure you say your name clearly.
- Be ready with your diary when making a follow-up call, in case they wish to organise an interview with you while you are on the phone.
- If it will help you to feel more comfortable on the phone, write out a script for yourself such as: 'Hi, my name is Amanda Rootsey. I was hoping to speak with John Hoodman, if he is available please? I'd like to follow up my application for the role of [insert role here].'

★ Get the job, every time
The interview

For the company, the interview is an opportunity for them to assess your personal qualities, work-related skills and communication skills, to see if you would be a good fit for their organisation. For you, the interview is an opportunity to market yourself to the employer, assess whether you would actually like to work there and show them why you are the best person for the job.

Tips for a great interview:

- Do your research beforehand—who works there, what are their values, what do they wear, what do they expect from you, etc.
- Turn up early and make sure you know where you are going ahead of time.
- Dress and do your hair and make-up appropriately for the job (make an effort to look like you belong there).
- Take your résumé (even though they have it).
- Make sure your references know that you are going for a job interview, in case they get a call.

- When you walk in, remember your posture, your handshake and a smile. Even do this with the receptionist—remember everyone is equal and you should always treat people with respect and kindness.
- They will probably ask you to take a seat—just sit up straight and use this time to take a couple of deep breaths, saying to yourself: 'I'm here. I've done everything I can to get this job. If it's meant to be, then I will get it!'

Interview questions

Before you turn up to your interview, have a think about how you would answer some common questions, such as:

- Can you tell me a bit about yourself? (Remember this is an opportunity to give them something other than what is on your résumé.)
- What are your strengths?
- What are your weaknesses?
- Why do you want to work here?
- Give me an example of how you can work in a team.
- What are your goals for the future?
- What are you hoping to get out of this job?

Towards the end of the interview, they will usually ask you if you have any questions. If you don't have any, just answer: 'No, I think you've answered them all for me, thankyou.'

Communication

Your suitability for a job will be largely determined by how well you communicate during the interview. If two people are being interviewed for the same job and one is a straight-A student who finds it difficult to talk to the interviewer, and the other doesn't look as great on paper but communicates well, then the second person would be likely to get the job.

Remember these tips:

✓ Practise active listening—nodding, making eye contact, encouraging verbal utterances like 'ah-hah' or 'I see.'
✓ Don't interrupt.
✓ Always be honest.
✓ Take a moment to think before you speak.

With all this in mind, you'll get a job in no time!

TIME MANAGEMENT + STUDY SKILLS

You can't be great at everything. And while we all want straight As, you're not going to be a mathematician, writer, biologist, musician, fitness instructor, physio, historian and artist in one lifetime. You might, but it's highly unlikely! So take the pressure off yourself to be the best at everything. If you do really well in your exams, **great**! But if not, don't undermine your hard work and self-confidence by berating yourself and putting yourself down. Learn what you can and move on.

Often, how well we do in exams and schoolwork comes down to how organised we are. The great thing about school is you can use this time to test out how you work best. If you ever want to work for yourself, be a company manager, a professional sportsperson or a reality TV star (whatever floats your boat!), then you'll need to be self-sufficient. You'll need to be able to get stuff done, without parents or teachers constantly telling you off. At no other time in your life will you be totally supported to test out what works for you and create habits that can last a lifetime, than right now at school.

You are a creative, spiritual, beautiful soul. Pay attention to your intuition. Listen closely. Trust yourself. Then do what feels right. Keep writing and expressing yourself. You have special gifts to share with the world. Don't be afraid to share them.

Megan Dalla-Camina, author of *Getting Real about Having it All* and *Lead Like a Woman* on what she'd share with her teen self

Extra Info! ➜ What's your learning style? We all learn in different ways—visual, auditory or kinaesthetic. If you're a visual learner then you need to **see** things, **read** the instructions and **watch** a demonstration. if you're an auditory learner then you need to **hear** the instructions, **talk** through options and have things **explained**. If you're a kinaesthetic learner then you love to learn by **doing**. You **move** around a lot, fiddle with pens and need to give things a go.

You probably already have an idea of what your learning style is but there are free quizzes you can take online to find out too. We've got one at www.shinefromwithinhq.com

Once you know your learning style you can set yourself up properly, both at school and when you're studying at home. For example, I'm kinaesthetic so sitting on an exercise ball at my desk at home helps me to stay focused, because I can bounce up and down a bit to keep myself moving. I'm also aware that I chew my nails if I don't have anything to do with my hands, so I try to play with my earrings and have a pen or stress ball to play with too.

★ Stress less

Everyone gets stressed. It's the way our bodies protect us, when we're in real danger. But being in a constant state of stress is unhealthy. Stress effects **everything**—from our skin, to our mood, to our ability to digest foods properly.

And there is not a time in your life when you won't have something to stress about. So the sooner you find ways to deal with stress that work for you, the more Zen your life will be.

How we react to stress is different for everyone. Depending on your personality type, you might get stuck in your head, overthinking everything and coming up with stories of what **could** happen (but what if I get to the party and there's a Dementor from Harry Potter or 'A' from Pretty Little Liars after me?), especially if you've discovered you're a Precise person. You might start snapping at everyone who comes near you (your poor, poor little bro!). You might get moody and go quiet, leaving everyone around you wondering what they did wrong. Your heart might race, your palms get sweaty and your mind go blank.

We've been training for this very moment. The best way to deal with stress is to understand more about who you are and get your building blocks to shine and self-care plan into action! Review parts 1 and 2 of this book for all the help you need.

Fill your cup first.

Michele Santo, founder of *Unstoppable Girl Squad*,
on what she'd share with her teen self

★ Plan like a pro

- Be disciplined. In order to live a gentle, happy life, you have to be disciplined, so you can get stuff done. Then you can play. Use your wisdom to do this in a way that works best for you.
- Always write out your to-do list for tomorrow the night before. Pick out the top three Most Important Tasks (MITs), so you start with those and don't waste an hour trying to get going.
- Ask yourself, 'What can I do today, to make life easier for myself tomorrow?'
- Keep a diary/calendar (just one) for everything and consult it regularly.
- Forgive yourself and be gentle with yourself. The crazy thing about being a teen is that you have so many responsibilities and deadlines but your brain isn't fully developed yet, so you physically have trouble remembering things or thinking about the consequences of your actions. So if you make a boo-boo, forgive yourself, try to learn from it and move on.
- Get at least nine hours sleep every night. Teens who get this often have higher grades.
- Add 25% more to your time estimates for projects as a buffer. So if you think an assignment will take you 2 hours to finish, give yourself 2½ hours instead.
- Break your projects up into mini deadlines, eg. essay plan on Monday night; fill in the body of essay by Friday; write introduction and conclusion by following Monday; edit/review by Friday week.
- Find out what works for you in terms of study and creation time. If you work best later at night, then have some downtime in the afternoon and study later at night. If you work best straight after school or first thing in the morning, then schedule your days accordingly.

Be productive, not just busy

It's easy to look busy and tell our parents we've been studying for six hours. It doesn't matter what we've achieved in that time, we're like 'Yep, I just studied for six hours; I deserve ice cream,' even if we've spent most of that time on YouTube. So switch from thinking in terms of time and have specific goals you need to achieve.

✓ Schedule reminders on your phone that pop up during study time and say something like: 'Am I being productive or just busy?'

✓ Don't multi-task—you just end up doing not much of a whole bunch of things and never get anywhere fast. Pick **one** thing (even if it's not an entire assignment, but part of it), finish it, and then do the next thing. Hint: Ten tabs open on your browser is not a great sign!

✓ One useful tool that I've found to manage time is the Pomodoro technique. Go to tomato-timer.com and start the 25-minute timer. Work on just one project during that time. When the timer goes off, do something fun for a few minutes, like put on your favourite song and dance like a lunatic. Then reset the timer and get back to work.

Plan your breaks

Have a list of things you'll do to refresh yourself, such as anything on your self-care plan and/or:

• colouring book
• walk, run or swim
• listen to music
• call your girlfriend
• do a yoga video

- pull all your clothes out of the wardrobe and try different things on
- declutter your bedroom
- go help your mum or dad with dinner

Try not to watch TV or scroll through social media during study breaks. These things just drain you further and don't recharge you. You need to be offline and peaceful in your mind. That's when you usually get a stroke of genius and can get back into study with renewed energy.

> *It's okay that you loved recharging your energy by spending time alone, when so many of your friends recharged by spending time with each other. This was just the start of you honouring yourself and your own needs!*
>
> Cassie Mendoza-Jones, best-selling author of *You Are Enough* and *It's All Good* on what she'd share with her teen self

★ Love to procrastinate?

Procrastination is when you do everything else **but** the thing you should be doing. I'm pretty good at it. For example, this book took way longer than it should have to finish! And while I'm glad about this, because it's perfect now and was released exactly when it was meant to be released, part of the delay was probably just procrastination. Let's get better at it, shall we?

Zen Habits suggests making time to practise and beat procrastination. Start by picking out **one task** to do and then:

1. Clear all distractions and get started (give yourself ten minutes to just focus on this one task).

2. When you notice the urge to switch to something more comfortable or do something else, pause and watch.
3. Notice how you're feeling, take a deep breath, then return to the task for the remainder of the ten minutes.
4. Repeat as many times as you need. At the end of the ten minutes, switch to something more comfortable.

Keep practising this and you'll create a habit of getting stuff done.

MONEY LOVE

★ Your relationship to money

*Every time you spend money, you are casting
a vote for the kind of world you want.*

Anna Lappe, author, educator and sustainable food advocate

You might not have thought about this before but it's so important to develop a good relationship with money now. And I say relationship, because you'll spend the rest of your life being dependent on it so you want to make it work for you!

Think about your best friend. You check in with her regularly and know what's going on in her life. If you need something, she's there for you and vice versa. If you were heading down a dangerous path, she'd let you know because she knows you—she knows your values, she knows what you stand for and she knows when you're not being true to yourself, even if it's hard to hear!

As we've already discussed in this book, you have to nurture good friendships or they fade away. You have to:

- be kind
- know what's happening in her life

- be real with her when she's not being herself, and . . .
- have some fun!

In the same way, you can nurture your relationship to money. Here are some suggestions:

- **Be kind**. Use positive language around money. Don't say 'I can't afford this' or 'money makes people snobs' or any other negative statement you may have heard about money.
- **Know what's happening** with your finances all the time. Don't stick your head in the sand, hoping you won't get declined at the checkout. #awkward Check your bank balance regularly, record what you're spending your money on and then regularly review this. For example, at the end of each month you could sit down and look at your bank statement and tally up how much you spent on clothes, food, travel and any other categories you can think of. This is fun because you get a clear picture of what's important to you, what you're happy to spend money on and where you might be able to rein it in a bit, so that you can save for something you really want. One less coffee/tea/juice each week can mean you'll have a few hundred dollars extra each year and you probably won't even miss it.
- **Give yourself a goal** of something to save for: a car, a dress, a trip overseas when you graduate. Get very clear on your goal, make it visual by putting an image of what you want up in your room or as the screensaver on your device, then work out how much you need to save each week to have it in your hot little hands.
- **Be real and honest** about your money situation. Once you know what's happening in 'moneyland' you can plan a bit better. You can budget, which is where you decide you'll

try to only spend (say) $100 a week on food, clothes and entertainment and save $20 each week towards your amazing goal. When you reach your budget, you then have to be strong and say: 'Actually I'm going to stay home tonight, but you guys have fun!'

Note: This only works if you've got a clear savings goal that you can remember in times like that. It's much easier to say 'I'm not going' when you have a picture of the car you want on your bedroom wall.

- **Have fun with money**—after all, lots of fun things do cost money! And when you earn your money, you deserve to do fun things with it, just not with all of it. It's all about balance and spending money on things you value, not just blowing it on food that makes you feel gross!

Money should support your survival and add value to your life, not make it extra stressful. For example, if you value freedom then you might be happy not to earn as much money, so that you have more flexibility on your weekends to have fun. Alternatively, you might devote yourself to more shifts, because you want to save up and go travelling. Make a conscious decision, then make it work for you.

★ Take shine-worthy action

1. Consider the following questions:
   - What's your relationship to money? How do you feel about it?
   - What kind of language do your parents use about money?
   - How does that impact on how you see money?

Write it all down here.

....

....

....

....

2. Start a list on your phone or download a free budgeting or money tracker app, then get into the habit of recording everything you spend. Next, schedule a regular time in your calendar to go through your bank statement or list from your phone, to work out where you've spent the greatest amount of money.

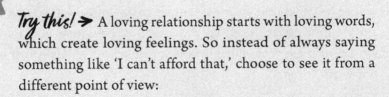

Try this! ➤ A loving relationship starts with loving words, which create loving feelings. So instead of always saying something like 'I can't afford that,' choose to see it from a different point of view:

- Can you save up for it and will it be more exciting when you get it?
- Are you meant to have it in your life right now? Do you really need it?
- Can you find a way to get it—sell something, get a job?
- Can you choose to value something else instead, or find something else to satisfy you, without buying that particular thing?

⭐ Money rules to live by

1. Spend less than you earn! Earning more doesn't mean you'll have more money. It rarely works that way, because we tend to just spend more.
2. Live joyfully and abundantly within your means. You have everything you need.
3. Spend money in line with your values. Invest in stuff that means something to you.
4. Think before you buy something, especially when shopping with friends. And make sure your purchase makes you feel good long term—not just for a few seconds!
5. Pay attention to your money. Get some kind of budget in place and take note of where you spend your money. You should always know how much money is in your account.
6. Pay yourself first. Every time you get paid from work, schedule an amount (even if it's just $10) to go into a savings account that you don't touch. You'll find a way to pay your phone bill and other bills, but make sure you put an amount away for you too.
7. Avoid getting yourself into unnecessary debt. I don't have a credit card, a car loan or a mortgage. And because I have no debt, I feel free baby! Not many adults can say that and, of course, we're all in different situations. But particularly while you're young, resist the temptation to get a credit card, store card, Afterpay or any kind of loan, just to get something faster. There's joy in waiting.
8. Find a cause you believe in to support. It doesn't matter how much money we have, we can always give a little.

A DREAMY SPACE TO SHINE

★ *Your bedroom is your temple*

Consider your bedroom as your holy, sacred, divine, super special space. The space where you get away from it all. Share a room? Your bed, your side of the room, your desk, your nook under the stairs, your tree house . . . whatever you have that is your space—claim it!

A little bunch of flowers (or even weeds!) picked from the garden that make you smile as you walk in; turning on your fairy lights that hang from the bunk above you—these small things can make you feel like you're in your own space. And in a world that feels like it's always wanting something from us, where we are constantly 'connected,' it's little things like this that help us feel nurtured and recharged.

Ten ways to turn your space into an inspiring cave that just oozes **you**!

1. **Find some quotes** that motivate you or make you smile and put them up on your wall. You could print them off or get crafty and write/paint/collage them.
2. **Declutter.** Go through your notebooks, drawers, boxes, wardrobe and anything else in your room and get rid of

whatever you no longer use or need. Donate it if you can, or throw it away. If you look around your room and feel overwhelmed about where to start with this, just pick one drawer or one corner of the room and tidy that space. Then, if you feel like it, move onto the next part. Just get started! As you work around the room, ask yourself: 'Have I **outgrown** this item?' 'Do I really **need** this item in my life or is it just taking up space?'

3. **Get organised.** Having a space for everything makes life easy and helps you feel calm. So now that you've made a bit more space by decluttering, give everything you own a home. Little things like making sure you have enough coathangers in your wardrobe can make a big difference and will make it easy for you to hang your clothes back up (after trying on ten outfits before walking out the door). You might like to install a couple of hooks behind your door, on the wall or behind the wardrobe door, so you can hang up favourite bags, scarves or a jacket that you use regularly.

4. **Clear out under your bed**. Feng shui (a Chinese philosophy of creating harmony with your environment) suggests that it's best to keep the area under your bed completely clear. But that might not be possible (so much great storage room!), so start by making sure it's clean and tidy under there. Pull everything out, vacuum and then, if possible, don't store things under there that mean a lot to you or have a history. This will help you to have a calm and restful sleep. Ideally, you can store clean bedding and pillows under your bed, but boxes full of old memories, shoes, technology and schoolwork you're still completing are all examples of things that could disturb your sleep.

5. **Decorate your room** with peaceful colours and vibes.

6. Before going to bed, **turn off all lights, switches and technology.** Get yourself an old-fashioned alarm clock if

you need, rather than have your phone next to your bed at night.

7. **Have a dedicated space for study.** This doesn't need to be your own desk or personal office (I wish!) but can be just a nook, shelf or cupboard where all your school stuff lives. Then when it's study time, find somewhere where you can sit at a table to work. As I said earlier, studies have shown that lying around on your bed while trying to study makes it harder for you to remember things, because your body is in relax mode. If you do have a desk in your room, make sure it's always tidy.

8. **Make it smell good.** I've shared my love of essential oils throughout this book, particularly in the skincare section, but oils can also be used around your bedroom. For example, you could get a little spritzer bottle, fill it with water and add a few drops of lavender. Spray this on your pillow for a restful sleep and all around your room to deodorise it regularly, helping it feel like a calm space. You could also get an essential oil diffuser (some plug into the wall, others are super cheap and you just light a candle in the bottom and add water and a couple of drops of oil in the top).

9. **Put up a to-do list** on a whiteboard or noticeboard in your room, so you always know what you need to do next. Or you could create a little binder, notebook or download a free app that's just for your to-do list; that way it's not staring you in the face when you wake up in the morning, but you know exactly where to go when it's study time to see what you need to focus on first.

10. **Use music.** Play music while you're decluttering and cleaning up. Play soothing sounds as you're getting ready for bed. Play study tunes in the background while you're studying. Music is so powerful—make it a part of your space.

As I've mentioned a few times throughout the book, ask yourself: 'What can I do today to help my future self?' Taking a moment to tidy your desk and write out what you need to do tomorrow before you go to bed helps you be relaxed and organised as soon as you wake up. I'm always talking about doing things for 'Future Mandy.'

And a bonus suggestion—make your bed each morning. A tidy bed is a magical way to start the day!

⭐ Take shine-worthy action

Pick at least one of the above points and get started!

PUTTING IT ALL INTO PRACTICE + LEAVING FEAR AT THE DOOR

~

★ A note from Issy

One of my beautiful past students has summed up the lessons in this book so beautifully:

> *Throughout my life I have been on a rollercoaster of a journey, trying to figure out who I am and the type of person I aspire to be. I finally came to the conclusion that truly being myself, being happy and having self-love were the most important aspects. I quickly realised that I didn't need to be like anyone else or always feel like I had to try to impress others. By doing this, I was able to attract the right group of friends, feel content with my life and find my true happiness.*
>
> *When I decided to do the things that bring me joy, I followed my heart and it has lead me on the most wonderful journey I could have ever asked for. I am currently enrolled in a degree that I absolutely love, I have*

adventured on the most amazing trips overseas by myself and am truly happy each and every day.

This all only fell into place once I started listening to my intuition. I would have loved to have told my younger self to not worry about what others thought and not feel like I had to fit in all the time. During my years at school, people thought I was strange and stuck up for always being focused and trying my best. But I chose to ignore these people and knew what was right for me and proved that I can do whatever I set my mind to. I was able to listen to my gut feeling by taking time out for myself—adding simple elements into my daily routine, such as meditation, yoga, walking and vision boarding.

I have also learnt that it is important to allow yourself to grow. Stepping outside your comfort zone allows you to develop as an individual and helps you to recognise that it's important to see the bigger picture in life, rather than worry about the little things like what others may think of you. If you take that courageous first step, you never know where it might lead you or what doors might open. By making the scary step to go travelling by myself, for example, I learnt that I have so much more resilience than I thought, made some wonderful friends and shared experiences that will stay with me forever.

⋆ Be gentle

> *In a gentle way you can shake the world.*
> Mahatma Ghandi, Indian politician, social activist and writer

Beautiful girl, you are perfect just as you are. Be gentle with yourself.

My wish for you is that you embrace who you are within and share your shiny self with the world. When you do that, the world will be a better place for all. I hope you feel strong, joyful, beautiful and know that you can absolutely chase your dreams. And in fact, you should. Because life can change in an instant and the world **needs** your awesomeness. So keep playing, exploring and shining your light in the world. Use your voice to speak out about causes you believe in.

May all the tools and tips in this book help you to shine from within.

> *I am so glad you were curious and brave—the adventures we had stay with me and inspire me now to keep taking the untrodden path; for no other reason than to experience new things.*
>
> Alice Jones, fashion designer, sharing what she'd tell her teen self

CONCLUSION

★ Final tips to #shinefromwithin

1. **Be kind.** Compassion for others looks gorgeous on you, darling! For me, that means being kind to all beings and treating everyone as an equal. If we can live a happy, healthy life without harming or putting down other people or animals, then why not? Being kind also extends to using the beautiful manners I know you have. And don't gossip. It's just a bit icky.

2. **Tread lightly** on this beautiful earth.

3. **Breathe.** When all else fails, a couple of deep breaths can instantly calm you down, lift your mood and help you put things in perspective. So often we breathe shallowly throughout the day, so taking a moment every day to consciously breathe deeply, down into our lungs, is magical. Like a unicorn.

4. **Do something for your future self.** If you can do one thing today that helps you tomorrow, then give yourself that gift. That could mean getting ahead on an assignment, so that you can feel more relaxed tomorrow. Or going for a run,

because you know it will make you feel happy and help you wake up tomorrow with a little more bounce in your step.

5. **Express yourself**. Journal. Write. Make art or music. Garden. Dance.

6. **Share your truth**. As we discovered earlier in the book, people who simply scroll and consume other people's lives on social media, instead of sharing their own, tend to have lower self-esteem than those who share actively. So stop watching everyone else and share your own awesomeness (mindfully of course). You know the rules - don't share anything you wouldn't share with your grandma!

7. **Nourish your beautiful bod**.

8. **Smile**. Not only does it physically change the vibes in your body to make you feel better, it usually makes someone else feel great too. Smile at a random stranger or the person serving you next time you're at the shops.

9. **Get out in nature**.

10. **Dream**. You can be, do, have, express, enjoy whatever you like in this life. Just not everything all at once! So dream your dreams and if you really, really want something—go for it. Give it your best and then let go and see what the universe has in store for you. Often it's even better than you could have imagined.

11. **Trust your gut**. That feeling you get in your tummy, your intuition, it knows stuff. Trust it. This can take time. Sometimes you feel a little nervous because you're doing something that will help you grow, which is a great thing. Sometimes you'll feel nervous about something because you know deep down you shouldn't be doing it. Check in with yourself and see which type of nerves you're feeling. You'll get to know which is which.

And don't forget, you can access a whole bunch of resources for free at shinefromwithinhq.com

Let nothing dim the light that shines within.

Maya Angelou, American poet, singer and civil rights activist

THANKYOU SO SO MUCH

This book has been made possible because I have an amazing group of people in my life. A dream is just a dream without taking action, believing it's possible and having people around you to share it with.

Thankyou David Rafter, my beautiful man, who has been my partner in life for over ten years. I love you and couldn't achieve anything in this life without your loving support. And of course our little fur baby, Trudi, I love you.

I couldn't have written this book without the inner guidance and connection to Heaven that I feel, thanks to spiritual teacher, Supreme Master Ching Hai. Since discovering your teachings, life has been magical beyond my wildest dreams.

Thankyou Hay House family . . . to get that call from Leon was a dream come true.

To my family, Mum, Dad, Michelle and Mark. Thanks for everything. I feel so blessed to have been born into our family and get to hang out in this life with you. To the Rafters, thanks for welcoming me so warmly into your family. Love you guys.

To my girlfriends, who inspire me, stretch me, give me a nudge when I need it and listen to me when I need to talk things out. Thank you. Especially Yvette Luciano, Nicola Newman,

Naomi Arnold, Jimilla Houghton, Rachel MacDonald, Tara Bliss, Nina Tovey, Melissa Ambrosini, Susana Frioni, Jess Ainscough (miss angel above) and all the beautiful women who contributed quotes for this book. I love you guys. And my schoolfriends, Ash, Jess, Karen, Sally, Michelle, Ashley, Yiota, Ealesy, Flynn and the rest of the 2001 cohort at Cannon Hill Anglican College—you guys made school easy and fun (most of the time)! I now realise how rare and wonderful that is. And to the teachers who encouraged us to be whoever we wanted to be, especially Mr Featherstone and Miss Betts—my English teachers—I never thought I'd have a book out in the world and wouldn't have been able to do it without you.

To my other teachers, past and present, who constantly guide me. Kelly Nahama, my first deportment teacher and employer in this youth field, this book would not be possible without you and the incredible opportunities you gave me. I certainly wouldn't be teaching girls to do their make-up or stand up tall without first learning it from you. Thank you. Julie Parker, for your constant inspiration and guidance and for teaching me how to be a life coach. Megan Dalla-Camina for helping me get strategic, while being patient and gentle with me. Kim Morrison, who I've learnt so much from, like the personality stuff in this book. You are always so much fun to work with. Yvette Luciano, I know I've thanked you already as a dear friend, but your constant support and cheering on in life and work encourages me to keep playing and trying new things.

To all of my students (and your amazing parents), I do truly love you. Thankyou for sharing a small part of your lives with me and giving me so much joy in my work. Your passion, enthusiasm for life, personality and seeing you embrace who you are, just as you are, are my greatest joys.

To the youth mentors who have trusted me to guide you on your journey, as you build your own beautiful businesses and programs to support teens in your communities . . . you guys blow me away every single day.

To my beautiful team: Brylie, Leah and the rest of the Shine From Within community, including our guest teachers, supporters and sponsors, venues, followers and volunteers . . . thankyou for constantly supporting us and helping us to do this work in the world.

LETTER TO MUMS AND DADS

~

Dear mum, dad, cool aunty or loving friend (or anyone else who is purchasing this for the young person they cherish) . . .

Thankyou for picking up this book. My hope is that it will help the young person in your life to shine a little brighter and be the very best version of themselves. But this is only the beginning. They need **you** to help them.

Some ways you can do that:

✓ Read the book too and ask them questions about it. 'What did you think about this?' Do it casually and then listen without judgement.

✓ Actively search for ways to support their curiosity and ways to express themselves, even if you don't absolutely love the direction they're going in. This is a time of discovering who they are. Knowing you love them, no matter what, goes such a long way.

✓ Schedule regular dates with your young person, whether that's a walk along the beach once a month, a day out once a month or a weekend away together once a year.

✓ Keep going. Even if your young person starts to pull away, make sure they always know you're there.

✓ Check out some of our free resources at shinefromwithinhq. com for more ways to support the young person in your life.
✓ Listen to our podcast 'The Youth Mentor Podcast' for short episodes with tips and a few laughs, from experts in this field.
✓ Send them along to one of our courses or book in for some one-on-one mentoring—we love bringing this content to life in person!
✓ If you want to work with young people yourself, check out our Youth Mentor Training to support you in creating your own curriculum and delivering programs for the youth in your community. Go to www.youth-mentor-training.com
✓ Trust yourself. You're doing the best you can. Keep going.

NOTES

....

....

....

....

....

....

....

....

....

....

....

....

We hope you enjoyed this Hay House book. If you'd like to receive our online catalogue featuring additional information on Hay House books and products, or if you'd like to find out more about the Hay Foundation, please contact:

Hay House Australia Pty. Ltd.,
18/36 Ralph St., Alexandria NSW 2015
Phone: +61 2 9669 4299 • *Fax:* +61 2 9669 4144
www.hayhouse.com.au

Published in the USA by:
Hay House, Inc., P.O. Box 5100, Carlsbad, CA 92018-5100
Phone: (760) 431-7695 • *Fax:* (760) 431-6948
www.hayhouse.com® • www.hayfoundation.org

Published in the United Kingdom by:
Hay House UK, Ltd., Astley House, 33 Notting Hill Gate,
London, W11 3JQ • *Phone:* 44-203-675-2450
Fax: 44-203-675-2451 • www.hayhouse.co.uk

Published in India by:
Hay House Publishers India, Muskaan Complex,
Plot No. 3, B-2, Vasant Kunj, New Delhi 110 070
Phone: 91-11-4176-1620 • *Fax:* 91-11-4176-1630
www.hayhouse.co.in

Access New Knowledge.
Anytime. Anywhere.

Learn and evolve at your own pace
with the world's leading experts.

www.hayhouseU.com

Lightning Source UK Ltd.
Milton Keynes UK
UKHW040756161118
332438UK00001B/49/P